the
art and
craft of growing
orchids

the
art and
craft of growing
orchids

leslie bowen

G. P. Putnam's Sons
New York

Library of Congress Catalog Card Number: 75–39781

SBN: 399–11736–9

Designed and produced by Walter Parrish International Limited,
London

Designed by Stephen Chapman
Drawings by Edward Russell

Set in 11 on 12 pt Apollo

Printed and bound in Spain by Talleres Offset Nerecan S.A., and
Roner S.A., Madrid

D.L. SS 161/1976

Foreword

It has been a privilege to read the manuscript of *The Art and Craft of Growing Orchids* and this work can be heartily recommended not only to those who are inquisitive and want to know 'what an orchid is', but also to the many thousands of amateurs requiring encouragement, guidance and additional information regarding their chosen hobby.

I have known Les Bowen for many years and have always admired the dedication and patience he has shown in answering the almost unending flow of questions put to him during the years he has served as secretary of The Orchid Society of Great Britain and also at the numerous orchid shows he has helped to organize.

This work is the culmination of the knowledge gained during many year's love of his subject and is certain to encourage readers everywhere to start growing orchids. They will never regret it and the friendship and pleasure they will gain from the peoples of the world will be an unbelievable experience.

My very best wishes for the success this publication deserves.

ERIC E. YOUNG

PRESIDENT, ORCHID SOCIETY OF GREAT BRITAIN
PRESIDENT, BRITISH ORCHID COUNCIL
MEMBER OF ROYAL HORTICULTURAL SOCIETY ORCHID COMMITTEE
AMERICAN ORCHID SOCIETY EDUCATION AND RESEARCH, AND CONSERVATION
    COMMITTEES
LANKESTER GARDENS COMMITTEE
WORLD ORCHID CONFERENCE COMMITTEE

Contents

Preface

Unless we are extremely careful future generations will be unable to enjoy many of the beautiful orchids we see today. Already many hardy species such as *Cypripedium pubescens, C. reginae, C. acaule,* and *C. calceolus* are disappearing fast in the USA; and in Great Britain *Orchis maculata,* and *O. fuchsii,* now renamed *Dactylorhiza,* as well as *Ophrys apifera* (bee orchid), *O. apanifera* (spider orchid), and *O. muscifera* (fly orchid), are almost extinct. They are almost impossible to transplant, or raise from seed away from their natural habitat. A few highly secret stands of Cypripediums and Orchis exist but these are at last protected by law and it is a punishable offence to move or pick the flowers. If this is happening to the orchids growing naturally in Britain and America, what of the more exotic species that we grow in our greenhouse?

Many hundreds of acres of natural habitat are being eliminated every day; man in his advance is destroying much of his own heritage.

Fortunately a few far-sighted people are fighting to stop this mass desecration. We can help in our way: we can join our various orchid societies, join forces with the professional nurserymen, and back the conservationist. Already the American Orchid Society and the Orchid Society of Great Britain have their conservation committees, and the A.O.S. has taken steps to preserve areas such as the Lankester gardens in Costa Rica. Much research is being done on raising rare plants by seed, and so on.

If many more species can be raised from seed this will cut down their importation from natural habitats and if this approach is encouraged all over the world, orchids will stand a better chance of being established once again in their natural home.

Remember, Man's love of orchids started their decline; it is up to us to do something to save them.

I hope this book will make a contribution in bringing a greater awareness of the possibilities of orchid-growing to a wider cross-section of plant-lovers than has generally been the case in the past.

My thanks are due to my many friends in the orchid world who have helped me pursue this fascinating hobby over many years; and to all the members of the staff of Walter Parrish International, in particular Timothy Auger, who have played a part in the preparation of the book.

LES BOWEN

1 The orchid mystique

What is an orchid? Are they poisonous? Can I grow them? Which ones? Will they grow indoors? I have been asked these and many similar questions while looking after the 'Gold Medal Exhibits' of the Orchid Society of Great Britain displayed at Chelsea, and at many other flower shows. They show that most people, including most experienced gardeners, are sadly lacking in knowledge and information about the culture of these fascinating plants.

There is, however, no reason why growing orchids should be a pastime for a privileged few—it is something that anyone can tackle. The aim of this book is to give you an insight into these plants and to penetrate the mystique that has grown up around them. With a little effort and surprisingly little money, you can enter the world of orchids. Most enthusiasts grow them in a greenhouse—and later in the book there is detailed information on the sort of greenhouse that is suitable. Orchids can also be grown in your home—either in an indoor enclosure known as a plantarium, or on a trolley inside a window. The aim of the book is to show you how.

People have always been attracted by fragrance and beauty; and so it is not surprising to find in early Eastern literature frequent reference to 'ran'. This is the Chinese for 'orchid'. The plants, mainly fragrant varieties, were cultivated by the wealthy in ancient China and Japan.

In early Grecian times the plants were given the name 'orkhis'. Literally, this means 'testicle', and the use of the name can be attributed to the shape of the swollen tubers of many orchids. They were believed to enhance virility and fertility, and it is interesting that in other parts of the world various native tribes had the same belief. Orchids have often had a part to play in religious ceremonies of one kind and another.

They are found in many scattered parts of the world, and stories which were circulated in the early 18th century by seamen and travellers returning from then-remote lands soon created a demand for them in the advanced countries of Europe. Very high prices were paid by the wealthy

OPPOSITE

Cattleya *Portia—this is a multi-flowered, award-winning hybrid carrying eight to ten 3" blooms on each spike.*

aristocrats of the day for any plants brought back. Large, costly collections were set up by men such as Sir Trevor Lawrence, William Bull, and Baron Schroder. Many of these collections still exist today.

Nurserymen such as Low, Veitch and Sander sent collectors out to look for orchid plants in all parts of the world; many of them—Arnold, Bateman, Boxall, Forget, Roezli, Warscewicz to mention a few—faced terrible hardship and danger from disease, wild animals and hostile natives to collect plants, and their names are remembered in horticultural history. For example, *Phalaenopsis boxallii* is named after Boxall, and *Zygopetalum warscewiczii* after Warscewicz.

Some of the plants sent to Europe fetched huge prices at the auctions, and in 1904 rare specimens are known to have fetched over £1400 (over US $3000)! *Paphiopedilum fairieanum* was lost for many years and a reward of £1000 (over $2000) was offered to whichever collector rediscovered it. There are many more such stories, and you can find them in *The Orchid King*, one of the titles listed later for Further Reading.

The taxonomy of orchids, that is to say, their botanical classification, was originally established by Karl Linnaeus, the 'Father of Botany', in the 18th century, when he classified orchids under the 'binary system' with the genus name followed by the species. The system of botanical names is explained more fully later in the book. Linnaeus was followed by John Lindley, who published *The Genera and Species of Orchidaceous Plants* in 1840. People such as Reichenbach and the Sander family have been adding to our knowledge ever since.

The methods used by those who went to find plants in the early days, however, had often disastrous consequences. As competition increased, so mass desecration of the jungles took place. Huge areas were destroyed by collectors, still mainly Europeans at this date, to prevent their rivals finding new species. Plants that had taken millions of years to evolve were destroyed. Possibly some of these held the key to our understanding of the evolution of the orchid, and have gone forever. Many thousands of plants died for want of knowledge on the part of those who packed them for the journey home. The long voyage was made by clipper, and many, many plants went to the bottom of the oceans. According to one report 21,000 examples of one species sank and perished in a single disaster. Many other specimens arrived home half-dead and those that still had life in them were soon killed in the very hot, steamy glasshouses that were thought to create the conditions to which the plants were accustomed. This led to yet more demand for plants, to replace those that were lost.

OPPOSITE
These different leaf shapes, characteristic of six orchid genera, show what variety evolution has produced. In general, plants with narrower, harder leaves, such as the Cymbidium, the Brassavola and the Vanda shown here, require more light than other, more fleshy forms.

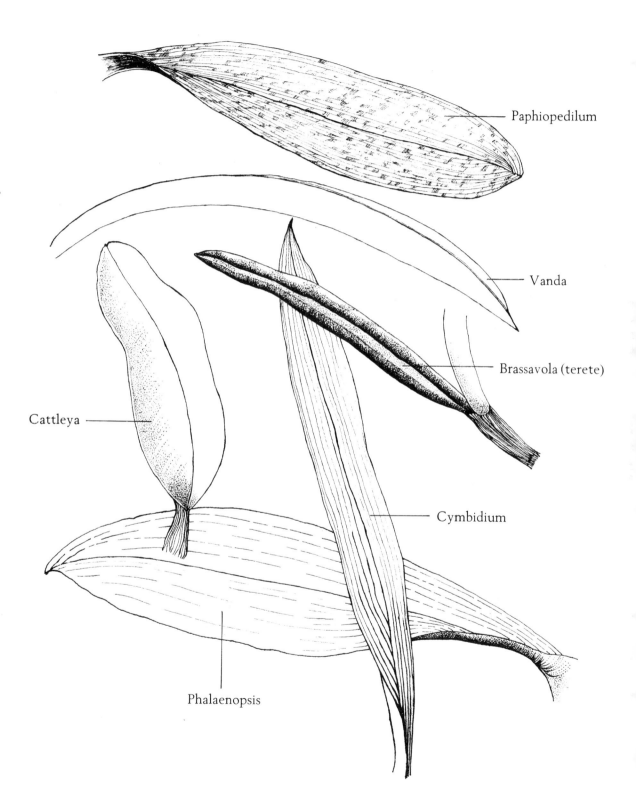

Paphiopedilum

Vanda

Brassavola (terete)

Cattleya

Cymbidium

Phalaenopsis

At last, in the 19th century, growers began to appreciate that creating the right conditions for orchids is not quite as simple as that. The credit is due to one man in particular—Joseph Paxton, a gardener to the Duke of Devonshire, who understood that plants from different parts of the world need different, and quite precise growing conditions—light, type of soil, air, and so on. Putting orchids in what was fondly, and wrongly, imagined to be a 'jungle' environment was not enough. What the early growers did not fully understand was that if the growing conditions are too hot—that is, continuously above about 82°F (28°C)—efficient photosynthesis stops, and so the chemical process which makes food for the plants to grow ceases. Likewise, too much sunlight will burn the tissues of the plants; this too leads to the failure of photosynthesis, and they gradually die. Over-hot, airless orchid-houses and the use of unsuitable materials for the plants to grow in, caused the demise of many species in the early days. Paxton approached the problem more scientifically, and set out to collect

Oncidium cheirophorum—*this fine specimen shows what the orchid-grower can achieve, and is of a standard likely to win cultural awards.*

from travellers and botanists more accurate information about the conditions in which orchids grew naturally. In many issues of *The Magazine of Botany*, in the period 1834–50, he wrote about his methods, which involved fresh air with less atmospheric moisture, different temperatures for different altitudes, and a more open, well-drained compost. The result was the successful growth of more plants. Many still perished but gradually conditions, and plants, improved.

For another twenty years the raising of new plants from seed was a complete mystery, and indeed many believed it impossible. Orchids differ from other plants in the amount of seed produced in a pod. The number can be anything from hundreds to over three million, and unlike what happens in other plants, this seed cannot germinate on its own, as it has no store of food. Simply sowing seed on various composts was a dismal failure. Then it was noticed that some seeds which had inadvertently been dropped onto a pot with an orchid growing in it had germinated. This was the key.

New plants—indeed all early new plants—were raised by sowing seeds on established plants. It was not understood why this should be necessary until A. B. Franks, a German botanist, discovered in about 1875 that the germination of the seed is dependent on the presence of a fungus relationship (symbiosis). The fungus concerned, mycorrhiza, penetrates the seed and provides the food for it to live on. Once roots are produced the fungus lives on these; thus orchid and fungus support one another. It is interesting to note that the orchid only allows the fungus to penetrate a certain distance into the root, being able to manufacture its own fungicide and keep the fungus in check.

Other breakthroughs were to follow. In 1865 the English grower John Dominy crossed *Calanthe masuca* with *Calanthe furcata* to produce the first hybrid, assisted by John Harris, an Exeter surgeon. In 1922 Dr L. Knudson, one of the early American pioneers, developed an agar, a sugar solution that enabled seed to be germinated in a laboratory. Since then hundreds of thousands of hybrids have been produced. In 1963 a further method of propagation was developed by the French Professor G. Morel, called 'meristem' culture. This entails taking the growing tip of a plant and growing it in a culture medium on a revolving wheel. It is dissected every so often and keeps proliferating so that thousands of identical plants can be produced from one tip. These plants are called 'mericlones'.

Through these different methods of propagation more people have been able to purchase orchids at fair prices, and more detailed and careful observation has led to a better understanding of the conditions needed for healthy growth.

2 Why are orchids different?

Orchids are the second largest Natural Order in the world of botany—they are known as the Orchidaceae. Estimates vary, but there are certainly over 700 genera and 15,000 species of orchid, displaying a stupendously wide range of characteristics—there are flowers of nearly every colour and shade, and tremendous variation in size and shape. Growth and natural habitat are just as diverse, and help to provide an exciting challenge for the intending grower.

The jungle is the home of most orchids. Perhaps this is part of their attraction. For most people there is a kind of lure in luxuriant foliage, exotic-looking plants, colourful birds and butterflies. If we look at the jungle more closely, we find, broadly speaking, that it stretches around the world between the tropics of Cancer and Capricorn, and is generally located on mountainous, coastal areas of land where moisture-laden winds from the seas create high rainfall and a moist atmosphere.

Jungle generally consists of tall trees, up to 150′ high, interspersed with a denser lower layer reaching to about 100′; beneath this grow trees and shrubs up to 40′ high with smaller plants below, down to the ferns and mosses on the ground itself. All of these are competing for the available light, water and food. Only a certain number of plants can be supported in a given area. The competition is fierce, so that over the millions of years during which plants have existed, they have adapted themselves so that their different requirements are met, and problems solved relating to light, temperature, atmospheric moisture, and physical and chemical make-up of the soil. This is what evolution is all about—plants have altered in some way so as to survive. In addition, mutations may arise and the original species disappear, making it hard to see how the different plants which have evolved were ever related.

In this fight for survival, orchids have developed many devices to perpetuate themselves, and often differ fundamentally from one another, for example in the way they find nutrition. We shall come back to this in more detail a little later on. Indeed, orchids differ so much from other plants in their shape, habit of growth, and flower structure, and there are so many differences between orchids themselves, that the beginner is often hard put to know whether the plant he has is really an orchid or not.

Botanically orchids are the most highly-specialised form of plant life. They are classified as angiosperms (flowering plants in which the seeds are contained in a closed ovary); angiosperms are divided into two groups with different basic features:

1. dicotyledons, plants that produce two seed leaves with multiple veining that grow from the top of the plant, and whose flowers are usually made up of five segments (although there are a few that are made up of four).

2. monocotyledons, plants that produce only one seed leaf with veins running always parallel, and shoots growing from the base of the plant. The flower segments are always in threes. Plants in this category are palms, iris, lilies, and grasses.

Orchids are also in this second group. Their flowers consist in part of three outer segments called sepals. These are not green like the sepals of other plants, that enclose the flower petals, but highly-coloured; they form part of the orchid flower. The other part of the orchid flower is the three petals. The orchid is again unlike other flowers in that one of the petals is different in size, shape, and colour from the other two. This petal is known as the 'lip', or 'labellum', and can take on numerous fancy shapes. Petals of most orchids are usually very thick and fleshy, and this gives the flowers a distinctive waxy, almost unreal, look.

The reproductive organs—stamens and pistils—are separate from one another in most flowers. In orchids they are joined together to make a single organ, which is called the 'column'. It contains the stamen, and the pollen. The pollen is in the form of a single, sticky mass, instead of the many individual grains of other flowers. The reason for this is that orchids have to produce a tremendous amount of seed to ensure perpetuation of the species; numbers of up to three million in a single seed pod have been counted.

To make all this seed, the pollen must first reach the stigma. The sticky pollen adheres effectively to the backs of the various insects which visit the flowers, and is then brushed onto the stamen. Highly-coloured flowers—either self- or bi-coloured, strong scents, single large flowers or a mass of sometimes hundreds; all these variations help to attract the various insects needed for fertilisation. Many intricate mechanisms have been devised by nature to achieve this, such as traps, hinged lids, mimicry and deception. The flowers may take on weird and wonderful shapes, and often mimic insects, assuming their shape, colour and smell so successfully that they fool the males of the species into false copulation. The insect, which carries the pollen then pollinates the orchid. There are bee and spider orchids, while some look like butterflies (see Oncidium), and some look like moths (see Phalaenopsis). Other systems to attract the insects have been developed; in some cases (e.g. Masdevallia) colourful petals containing nectar tip inward when the insect lands, thus pushing it onto the pollen. One petal of Coryanthes is formed into a bucket shape holding a sweet liquid to attract the insect, which slips into the bucket; when it manages to find its way out it passes the pollen which sticks onto its back. One species even supplies its own staircase—growing low down on the rocks or fallen branches, the petals of Phragmipedium reach down until they touch the ground, whereupon growth stops. They then act as a ladder up to the flower. Sometimes the petals extend to three feet.

Once fertilised, the flowers quickly wither, usually taking on a pinkish colour. The seed pods take up to eighteen months to mature. Some of these pods can reach a very large size—in Cymbidiums they may measure up to 5″ long and 1½″ in diameter. The seeds, almost microscopic and weightless when released, are blown in every direction—this is nature's way of preventing overcrowding. Unfortunately very few find the right conditions for germination.

The seeds of orchids cannot survive unless they are in contact with mycorrhiza, a microscopic filamentous fungus that lives in the soil and on certain trees. It penetrates the seed covering and supplies it with the food to start into growth.

This partnership is necessary to all types of orchid, all through the orchid's life, and is called 'symbiosis', living together. It is a form of co-operation in which both organisms benefit (whereas in true parasitism

The flowers of Lycaste aromatica, *clearly showing the formation of the lip.*

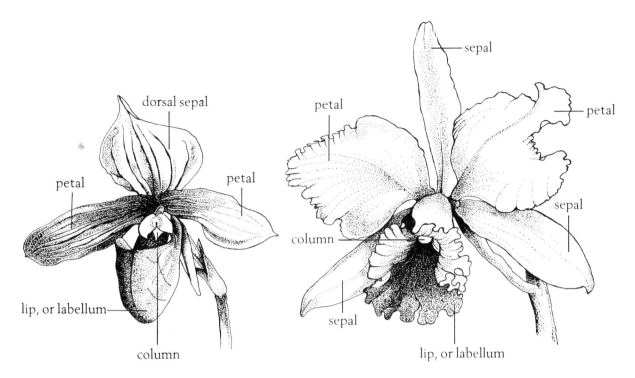

dorsal sepal

petal

petal

petal

petal

sepal

sepal

sepal

column

column

lip, or labellum

lip, or labellum

Typical flower shapes of the Paphiopedilum genus (left) with its characteristic lip, and of a Cattleya.

only one of the parties benefits, the other slowly dying). Two other examples of symbiosis in plant life are the association formed by the ordinary pea with bacteria that colonise in nodules on the roots of the pea, take nitrogen from the soil and turn it into nitrates; and secondly the habitation of ants inside the hollow stems of plants which they protect by attacking any animal grazing nearby, thus saving the plant from destruction. In return they receive food and shelter, living on the sugar exuded by the plant.

Orchids can be split into three growing classes, the main difference between them being the way in which they obtain food, moisture and light from their surroundings.

1. The saprophytic plants live on decayed vegetation and have no green leaves—they have lost the ability to manufacture their own food. One example of this group is *Corallorhiza innata*, an orchid that relies completely on the mycorrhiza fungus for its food. The saprophytic orchids are very few in number. Since they do not have very beautiful flowers, they are best disregarded by the beginner.

2. Terrestrial orchids grow in ground or marsh land. Strictly speaking these orchids behave as bulbous plants, dying down in the winter and sending up new growth in the spring. Examples are the British native orchids, Ophrys and Orchis. The group does, however, include two of the most popular genera, Paphiopedilums, the 'slipper orchids', and Cymbidiums, familiar in the bridal bouquet. These terrestrial orchids are evergreen and have thick hairy roots with a yellowish, bare tip.

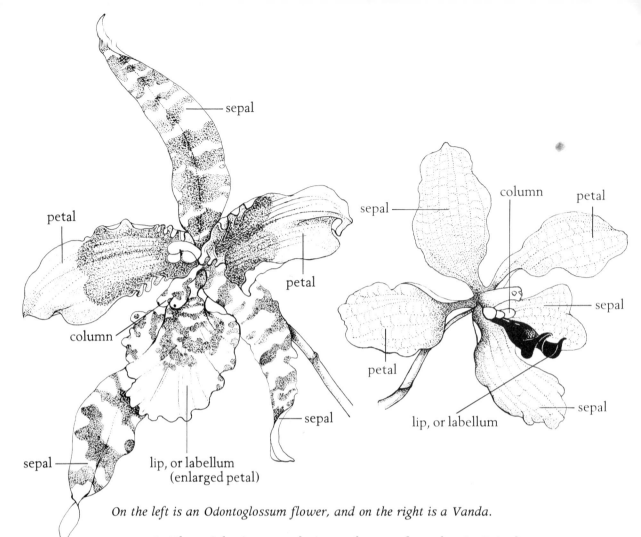

sepal

petal

petal

column

sepal

lip, or labellum
(enlarged petal)

sepal

column

petal

sepal

petal

sepal

lip, or labellum

sepal

On the left is an Odontoglossum flower, and on the right is a Vanda.

3. The epiphytic group derives substance from the air. It is the largest group by far, and has given up competing for light and food on the forest floor, and grows mainly on rocks and trees.

Nearly all plants need light to make food. This is done by a process called photosynthesis. By means of the chlorophyll in the green parts of plants, light and energy is used to turn water and carbon dioxide into glucose and starch (carbohydrates). These compounds make the new tissue to enable plants to grow, while at the same time oxygen is released through the leaf pores. When darkness comes this process is reversed, and carbon dioxide is given off. The production of oxygen is most important to man, and to all living things—without the replacement of oxygen in the air all life would soon end. It is in the quest for light that the epiphytic orchids have taken to the trees, while some cling to rocks or hang on the sides of cliffs or river banks.

The epiphytic orchids have developed a unique root system, quite unlike that of other plants, which helps them to hold, climb, and take up nourishment. These roots can be thin and wiry, or thick and quite stiff. Round, or flat like ribbons, the roots are distinctive in that they are covered in a layer of dead silvery tissue, called the velamen, which absorbs moisture to be used by the plant. The roots have a bright emerald-green tip, and hold quite strongly to the trees and rocks and of course to pots, both inside and out—indeed, they are difficult to remove without breaking. The tip is up to $1\frac{1}{2}''$ long, when the plant is growing well and receiving the correct proportion of light, food, etc. It contains a large amount of chlorophyll and therefore can assimilate food by photosynthesis.

Some recent experiments have proved that the root can do this even better than the leaves themselves. When the plant is resting, the root tip is completely covered by the velamen which protects it from excessive light and heat. There is a theory that fumes rising from the decaying vegetation on the jungle floor feed these roots under natural conditions. This I doubt, as most decaying matter gives off methane, which is not particularly beneficial to plant life. It is more likely that the roots are fed by volcanic dusts and the like, rich in minerals and distributed by the

A fully terrestrial plant, such as this Cymbidium, puts roots down into the compost in order to gain nutrition.

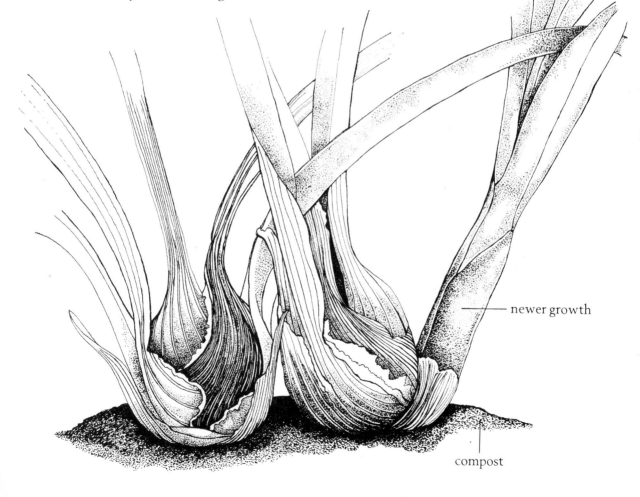

newer growth

compost

aerial roots

This Vanda shows how an epiphytic plant throws out aerial roots. Sometimes, as in this case, the plant will also put roots down into the compost, but this is as much to hold itself steady as for the acquisition of food.

winds and the rains. Like any other plant, an orchid is only as good as its roots, and care must be taken not to damage them. On some varieties the aerial roots can be up to three feet long.

One of the main concerns of epiphytic orchids is the storage of water and food. This accounts for the variations in stem growth. Some have egg-shaped swollen stems, some club-shaped, some thin cane-like growths with thick fleshy leaves, and others have thick, wide leaves with hardly any visible stem. Nature has adapted them all to suit different climates and conditions in the areas where orchids grow.

OPPOSITE
The varied forms of stems, or pseudobulbs, which have evolved in response to different conditions. Pseudobulbs are not bulbs proper, but storage organs for food and moisture.

cane-type pseudobulb
(Dendrobium)

egg-shaped pseudobulb
(Coelogyne)

reed-type pseudobulb
(Epidendrum)

If we look carefully at all the variations they will give us an insight into the cultural requirements of each type of orchid, whether epiphytic or terrestrial. We find there are two main growth patterns. In the first the plant stem grows upright with very few side growths. These plants can throw out roots anything from an inch to four feet from the base; the flower spikes can come from the centre, side or top of the stem; and the leaves are usually opposite one another or alternate. Some varieties grow only 6″ high, others can go to 30″ or more. New growths develop from the base, or stem of the plant, or even from the end of the flower spike. Examples of this growth pattern are the popular slipper orchid and the vanilla of commerce. These orchids are known as 'monopodial'.

The other type grow forward by means of a connecting stem, a 'rhizome', which sends up bulb-like stems called pseudobulbs. This type is known as 'sympodial'. These pseudobulbs, although some of them look like bulbs proper, are really just storage organs for moisture and reserves of food and come in a variety of shapes. The plant's leaves grow from the top of the pseudobulb and new growths from eyes, dormant buds at the base of each pseudobulb. The flowers themselves can come from the base, side, or top. Some of the pseudobulbs are shaped like clubs, ranging in size from 1″ to 2′ or more in height. Others are egg-shaped, and 6″ high. Others again have long reed-like stems up to 5′ high, like the genus Sobralia which, when out of flower, can easily be mistaken for a clump of bamboo. Many sympodial orchids have rhizomes so short that there does not appear to be a join between the individual bulbs—but nevertheless it is there.

Leaves in their turn vary tremendously in size, shape and texture. They are generally of a dark, rich green; a few are beautifully patterned

The upward growth pattern known as 'monopodial'—in this case a Paphiopedilum.

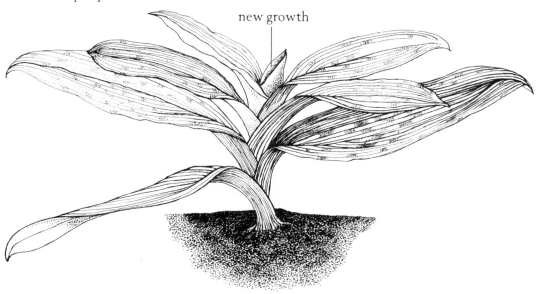

new growth

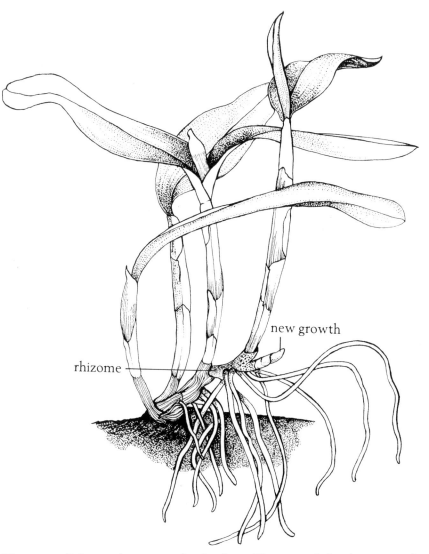

The sympodial growth pattern of a Cattleya. New growth develops towards the light.

with light and dark mottling. Some have richly golden, veined areas and one variety, Macodes, the jewel orchid, has brownish-green leaves with brilliant red and copper lines.

Leaves can be thick, leathery, wide, narrow, soft, plicate or cylindrical, and are normally entire (no serrations or wavy edges). The different leaf types vary in the amount of light they should receive. Leathery leaves will put up with more than soft ones, large fleshy types less than thin ones. The less light required, the softer and broader leaves become, and the amount of light needed will be a factor in determining how high off the ground a plant grows.

3 How to set about it

The most popular orchids grown today fall into roughly seven groups: Cymbidiums, Paphiopedilums, Cattleyas, Dendrobiums, Odontoglossums, Phalaenopsis and other genera. Although the beginner in his early enthusiasm acquires some of each, he soon finds out that although they will grow together, they each need different sets of conditions if they are to flower satisfactorily. As I have explained, the temperature can be too hot as well as too cold.

So one of the first things you have to decide is, how seriously are you going to take your orchid-growing? I am not trying to suggest that, without a lot of money, a great deal of space, and endless time and energy it's not worth starting. This is quite wrong. You can grow orchids outdoors in a specially designed and constructed greenhouse; but equally, you can grow them indoors, either in a glass case known as a plantarium, or even, if you select one of the plants which are less demanding of growing conditions, on the window sill of your bathroom or kitchen. While there are many people for whom growing orchids is a passion, don't imagine that you have to make it a full-time occupation in order to achieve anything. Given care, and the right conditions, anyone can grow a few orchids.

But you have to decide broadly how you are going to go about it, because that will have a bearing on what plants you decide to grow. So let's have a very brief look at the different basic approaches, which will be dealt with in more detail in the next chapter.

To grow orchids outdoors, we will need an open-sited greenhouse, away from any trees or other obstructions that can block out the natural light.

To create conditions as near as possible to Nature, we have to supply our plants with heat, light, water, air and food. These ingredients are not financially embarrassing, except perhaps for the one that concerns us most—heating. This is the number one priority and should be considered most carefully. The climate must never be underestimated. It is a false

OPPOSITE
The view inside an amateur orchidist's greenhouse. The epiphytic roots of several orchids are very obvious, bottom left. In the centre of the picture are specimens of Epidendrum and Dendrobium.

economy just to plan for a minimum outside temperature of 5°F below freezing, and take the risk of the occasional temperature dropping to 10° below. A whole collection can be ruined on that one night. A little extra money spent in the beginning can save years of work. Of course, over a vast continent like North America, much greater extremes of temperature than this are regularly encountered, and the best way to find out the coldest temperature to expect is to contact your local weather centre.

So, first and foremost, you have to be sure that your heating apparatus can cope with any possible temperature drop. It's also advisable, if your collection is valuable, to have an emergency back-up system—so many things can and do go wrong, especially in these days of energy shortage. Then, of course, ventilation arrangements have to be adequate. All plants need a certain amount of fresh air, and air movement helps to keep the temperature down in over-hot conditions. Humidifiers, which disperse minute particles of moisture over the plants, help to do the same job.

The general principles of growing plants indoors are, as we shall see, similar to those for growing them in a greenhouse. Whether they are placed in a special plantarium or just grown near a window, the plants need moisture, air, and a temperature maintained within certain limits.

We can then decide what plants to grow. If we are able to keep a minimum temperature of 50°F (10°C) then we have a large choice of the cool-growing species and hybrids, such as Brassia, Coelogyne, Cymbidium, Dendrobium, Laelia, Lycaste, Maxillaria, Odontoglossum, Oncidium, Paphiopedilum and many more. A temperature of 55°F (13°C) allows us to grow even more Paphiopedilums, hybrid Odontoglossums, as well as many other plants of the cool-growing category. A temperature of 62°F (16°C) extends our range to the beautiful Cattleya, mottled-leaf Paphiopedilums, and the fabulous moth orchid, Phalaenopsis, and many more.

Obviously some of these categories will overlap—one can always find a cool spot where some of the lower-temperature bracket will fit in. But it is important that temperatures should be taken as absolute minimum levels.

Your first plant should be purchased from a reputable orchid nursery, or specialist orchid-grower, preferably at an orchid show. It should be in flower and your own choice. First, of course, make sure it will suit your conditions. Do not be afraid to tell the grower this is your first orchid—he will do his best to encourage you. Then, look around the show and join the orchid society that will invariably have a stand there. Your subscription will immediately put you in contact with other orchid-growers in your area, and lifelong friendships will be made. Help and advice will be given and almost certainly your collection will be increased by the plants given with this advice—orchid people are like that. Club meetings are usually held on a monthly basis. Lectures, practical demonstrations, and slide shows are held and plant exchanges and visits to nurseries help one to get the most out of one's hobby.

At the end of the book you will find the names and addresses of many national orchid societies; these will be able to supply you with the names of local societies or groups near where you live.

Plants themselves can be bought at the time of writing, 1976, for anything between £1.50 and £300 in Britain, all of flowering size and in all of the different genera, both species and hybrids. In the US prices start at around $5.00, and here too the sky's the limit. Some people are prepared to pay very high sums for plants of particularly fine merit, if they are connoisseurs, but a whole range of beautiful plants can be bought at prices which are no higher than those one would pay for garden shrubs. Further plants should be added at monthly intervals with

The spidery flowers of Brassia maculata, *originally from Jamaica. The dark-brown markings are clearly visible.*

at least one in flower. In this way a mistake often made by beginners is avoided—many get disheartened after months of looking at green leaves because they have bought unflowered seedlings, bare-rooted imports, or back-bulb propagations they are told should flower in a few months. Orchids are slow-growing plants and some seedlings take up to seven years to flower.

For the first year or two I think it is best to buy your plants in flower and preferably in only one or two genera. They should be ones that you and you alone like. This way you will grow to love them and nurture them. There will be plenty of time later to attempt others that could win prizes. We all have plants that others would not give house-room to, and vice versa. All orchids are beautiful in their own way, from those one has to view through a magnifying glass to the large exotic Cattleya. Fortunately our personal tastes differ, and we can be selective, otherwise we would never have a greenhouse large enough to hold them all.

Wishing to add to his stock, the novice orchid-grower should visit more shows and make notes of plants he wishes to have in the future. Let us suppose you see a large pink flower with a crimson lip. You immediately like the look of it, you cannot buy at the time, but you duly make copious notes about its size, and name. Crosses are given one name, for example 'Tom × Jerry'. What you may not have realised, however, is that this crossing may have produced thousands of plants. Some are sold as unflowered seedlings, others kept by the nursery. As soon as some flower, the nurseryman selects one or two of the best to exhibit at the next show. Genetics being what they are, every plant in the seed pod which produced the cross will be different in shape and colour. If you look carefully at the display you might well see, let us say, a nice *white* flower with a *pink* lip, also labelled 'Tom × Jerry'! The nurseryman unaware of your lack of knowledge, could well send you this plant in good faith, and you won't end up with what you were hoping for.

Again, the moral is, until you have gained a sound basis of knowledge, buy plants that you have *actually seen in flower*. If you see a hybrid plant, and you want to acquire an exact replica of it, ask the nurseryman for a 'division' or 'meristem' of that particular plant. Division will be explained in greater detail in Chapter Five.

4 Conditions for growing

If you have never tried to grow an orchid before, and you want to take up the hobby for the first time, it is unlikely that the first thing you will do is to spend a lot of money on a greenhouse specially designed and equipped for the purpose. Most people will want to start in a smaller way, probably indoors.

So you may wonder why, in a book aimed mainly at beginners, I am going to spend the first part of this chapter describing the ideal orchid-house, and all the facilities which should go into it. Over-ambitious, you may say. But it is a help to know how orchids are grown by people who go in for them in a big way, because then, with a bit of ingenuity, it is often possible to reproduce these conditions on a more humble scale. In any case, once you have acquired some knowledge of these unusual plants, it is more than likely that your enthusiasm will grow, and it is always useful to know how to take your hobby on to the next stage.

GROWING ORCHIDS IN A GREENHOUSE

To create the ideal conditions for growing a range of orchids, the enthusiast uses a greenhouse. If only a single greenhouse is available, it can be divided up by one or more partitions made of glass or polythene—in this way environments with different temperatures can be achieved. The exact type of greenhouse is not important—any sort can be used, from a humble home-made lean-to to a large aluminium structure specially bought for the purpose.

Any greenhouse has its limitations; how severe these are will depend on the depth of your pocket. In any case they can generally be overcome, with a little ingenuity.

The site for the greenhouse should be as open as possible, but at the same time sheltered from cold winds, for these can lower the temperature dramatically inside the greenhouse, and can be just as dangerous as a frost, if not more so. The best possible use must be made of whatever winter light is available, and so a north–south orientation is generally best, as this ensures that all the plants in the house get a fair share. Try and keep the greenhouse away from trees or other obstructions, and easily accessible from your house—it is worth avoiding long walks on cold, wet winter's nights. Bear in mind too that the greenhouse must be supplied with water, electricity for lighting, and heating fuel. Long runs of wire or pipe can be very expensive, and most oil-delivery vehicles only carry a limited length of hose-pipe.

The choice of materials is important too. Greenhouses of timber, plastic-coated steel, plastic, aluminium, concrete and brick are available commercially; few manufacturers, however, produce the ideal structure for the orchid-grower, and these usually only to order.

If you buy a greenhouse ready-made, remember that timber needs regular painting, and, over a period of time, is susceptible to rot. When you have to make structural repairs, it is not easy to find suitable temporary accommodation for a sizeable collection of orchids. With a timber structure, however, the fitting of shelves, hooks and wires and other attachments is comparatively easy.

Steel and aluminium are invariably stove-enamelled or plastic-coated and unless they are badly treated they are virtually rust- and rot-proof. They often have patented glazing systems that make the replacement of glass panels a pleasure, and so eliminate the chore of chipping away at hardened putty in the middle of winter. Extra fitments can be difficult to install; unfortunately those supplied by the manufacturers are never exactly where you want them. This can be a problem with concrete structures, too.

Brick-based greenhouses are a better proposition and should give one a lifetime of service.

Greenhouses with glass right down to the ground are not recommended unless you are to grow Cymbidiums only. Most orchids require top light only, and indeed the best type of greenhouse for the orchid-grower is one bricked or boarded up to the eaves. The advantage of this arrangement is the good build-up and retention of heat and humidity. If you are going to build your own greenhouse, this is one design to consider seriously.

Even better is the sunken house. Building it involves a lot of hard work. A pit must be dug at least five feet deep, and the walls built inside the hole, supporting the roof at ground level. A word of warning: care must be taken that flooding of the entrance and boiler housing does not occur in heavy rain. An effective drainage system is most important.

Houses constructed of plastic corrugated sheets have become popular recently. These are suitable for orchids provided they are securely anchored; unfortunately plastics do tend to deteriorate because of the action of sunlight and in this respect glass is far preferable.

No greenhouse is likely to be large enough for the grower bitten by the orchid bug. Start with the largest you can, and when you choose the site allow for the possibility of extending the greenhouse at a later date.

All materials used in the orchid house must be able to stand not only the excesses of the weather outside, but also the warm moist conditions that have to be created inside. These can be just as destructive.

Benches especially should be constructed of either aluminium or some other rot-proof material supported on stout piers. Square-meshed plastic is available and suitably supported with aluminium cross-pieces this allows for free drainage and air circulation. Don't forget to inspect the bench regularly even after plants are placed on it. A collapse spells disaster, a mass of labelless plants and smashed pots. The bench height should be about 2′ 9″, and width no more than 2′ 9″. Leaning over a wider bench than this to lift a plant from the back has cost growers many a fine plant. It is easy to let a plant slip from your fingers and drop onto your choicest specimen with disastrous results.

The same applies to gangways. The minimum safe width is 2′ 6″, unless you enjoy constant repotting. Paths should be laid with concrete, or wooden duckboards. Water-filled troughs of concrete, slate or polythene under the benches help considerably to create nice, moist conditions.

All greenhouses should be double-glazed. It has been estimated that this can save up to 45% of heat loss—a fact that seems to have escaped most manufacturers. However, you can achieve your own substitute to some extent, by lining the whole of the greenhouse with polythene sheeting, stretched tight and 2″ away from the glass, so as to trap a still layer of air between the sheeting and the glass which helps insulate the house. There must not be any holes or gaps if the insulation is to be effective. Ventilators should be lined separately. This lining also has the advantage of preventing the loss of plants because of drips. No greenhouse made seems to be leak-proof. Leaks are insidious things which seem to stop as soon as you enter the house and start again as soon as you leave; they always seem to occur above your most expensive plants, with fatal results.

Ventilation should be of two types, in the roof and under the benching. Sliding box ventilators should be set 12″ above floor level on both sides of the greenhouse to allow incoming air to be warmed before blowing over the plants and to prevent the temperature from dropping suddenly. Low-level ventilation has the advantage that humidity is more easily controlled. All ventilator openings should be covered with a material such as very fine plastic mesh, or gauze, to stop the entry of bees, and other insects, including many pests. Periodic checking for draughts and drips should be made.

Heating is probably the orchid-grower's main worry. Reliability has to be combined with economy. Alas, one only gets what one pays for: the aim is a reliable supply of controllable heat, with ease of maintenance and minimal running cost.

Gas, electricity, oil, solid fuel, all have their advantages and disadvantages, but each will only give a known quantity of heat for a given price. Heat always flows from the higher to the lower temperature and so in cold weather from the inside to the outside of the greenhouse. The rate of flow depends upon the insulating properties of the greenhouse materials, the site and the temperature difference. Depending upon which orchids we wish to grow, we have to maintain a certain minimum night temperature—perhaps 50°, 55°, or 62°F, as against the expected outside minimum air temperature. If, for example, this is 20°F, you will need an increase of 30°, 35°, or 42°F.

Now all building materials have a known 'heat loss figure' which is used in calculating the necessary output of the heating equipment. For example, that of $4\frac{1}{2}''$ brick is 0·60, wood 0·50, glass 1·00, soil 0·33, concrete 0·60, double-glazed glass 0·50, asbestos 0·89; and if we multiply these figures by the area of the greenhouse walls in square feet, it will give us the required number of BTU (British Thermal Units) needed to raise the temperature of the greenhouse by 1°F. Multiply this by the estimated difference in temperature between inside and outside, and the total gives us a guide to the minimum size of heating equipment we need. Let us take as an example a $12' \times 8'$ greenhouse with $2'\,6''$ wooden walls and $2'\,6''$ glass sides; we want to keep the temperature inside the greenhouse at a minimum of 50°F, and the lowest outside temperature is estimated at 20°.

		Surface area of walls		Heat loss figure		
Wooden sides	$12' \times 2\frac{1}{2}' \times 2 =$	60 sq ft	×	0·50	=	30
Wooden ends	$8' \times 2\frac{1}{2}' \times 2 =$	40 sq ft	×	0·50	=	20
Glass sides	$12' \times 2\frac{1}{2}' \times 2 =$	60 sq ft	×	1·00	=	60
Glass ends bottom	$8' \times 2\frac{1}{2}' \times 2 =$	40 sq ft	×	1·00	=	40
Glass ends top	$4' \times 2' \times 2 =$	16 sq ft	×	1·00	=	16
Glass roof	$12' \times 5' \times 2 =$	120 sq ft	×	1·00	=	120
Earth floor	$8' \times 12' \quad =$	96 sq ft	×	0·33	=	32
						318 BTU

This means that to compensate for a temperature drop of 1°F, due to heat loss through the greenhouse walls, roof and floor, we need a heat output of 318 BTU. In our example we need to compensate for a possible

OPPOSITE
Oncidium crispum *is one of the larger-flowered Oncidiums—the 2″ spike will carry up to twenty 2″ chestnut-coloured flowers. This is a well-shaped example.*

temperature drop of 30°F, and so the heating apparatus must have an output of at least 9,540 BTU. To keep a minimum of 55° would require 11,130, and 62°, 13,356 BTU.

All fuels will produce a certain number of BTU when burnt: oil, 160,000 per gallon; solid fuel, 19,000 per pound; gas, 100,000 per therm; electricity, 3,412 per kilowatt; and 4″ hot-water pipes, about 200 BTU per foot. So for our 12′ × 8′ greenhouse kept at 50° we will require either: a 3-kw heater; or 50′ of tubes; or 48′ of 4″ hot-water pipe heated by a boiler fuelled by gas, oil, or solid fuel; or a 2″ burner oil heater, burning 1 gallon in 24 hours. It is possible in a similar way to work out heating requirements for any greenhouse in relation to the expected minimum outdoor air temperature, wherever you live.

What other factors come into the choice of heating equipment? As electricity is invariably installed for lighting, extra equipment for heating is usually easily fitted and is very efficient. Fan-heaters have the advantage of even distribution of heat and the moving air is beneficial to

Some of the facilities in the amateur orchid-grower's ideal greenhouse.

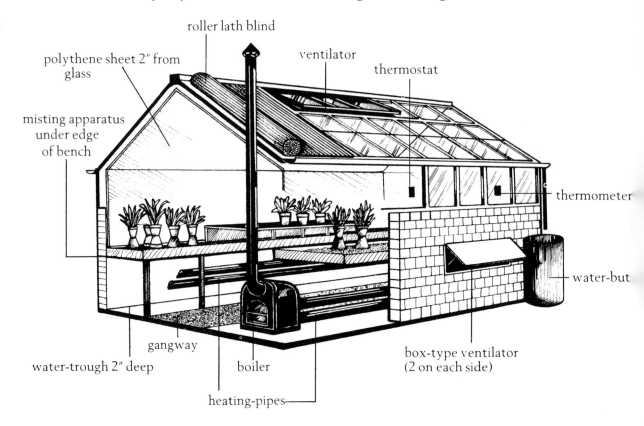

the plants. Electric tubes can get rather hot and create dry areas and so plants must be protected from them. Copper water-cylinders heated by an immersion heater are useful for smaller greenhouses. Whatever type of electric heating is used, a good rod-type thermostat should be used to ensure economic use of it, and all fitting done by a qualified electrician.

Oil can be used to heat hot-water systems or in freestanding heaters. These are very inexpensive to install but they are apt to fill the pathway as they should not be placed under plants or benches. Scrupulous cleanliness must be observed and wicks trimmed properly, otherwise fumes can affect the plants; but used intelligently these heaters are most economical—I have grown orchids for twenty years using two of them. Care must be taken to ensure that the greenhouse is not completely sealed, otherwise the heater will go out. A small sliding vent, 8″ × 4″, fitted in the bottom half of the door, is sufficient. Gas is an economical and reliable means of heating, and thermostatically-controlled units are available.

A hot-water boiler with 4″ pipes, although one of the oldest means of heating a greenhouse, still remains one of the best, giving an even, continuous heat; the boiler can be either inside or outside the greenhouse and the fuel can be coal, coke, oil, gas or electricity. My own preference is for a boiler with 4″ hot-water pipes fitted with an oil-firing conversion unit and a thermostat, together with a 3-kw immersion heater set into the pipes. This has the advantage that one can buy oil yearly, and so ensure a year's supply. If any mechanical faults develop, the immersion heater will take over; it will also be a supplementary heat source on unusually cold nights. If oil is unobtainable the conversion unit can be quickly withdrawn and solid fuel used. This does present slight storage problems but at least one has peace of mind for twelve months, and the whole of the summer to find the next year's supply of fuel.

Boilers can be driven by solid fuel alone, but these require constant attention and stoking every 24 hours.

Fans, humidifiers, and time switches are commercially available, and can all help towards complete automation, but one should not perhaps make things *too* easy, for this takes much of the satisfaction out of one's achievements. Besides, you can save a great deal of money by devising your own solutions to simple problems.

GROWING ORCHIDS IN THE OPEN

If you are fortunate enough to live in a part of the world where ambient temperatures are suitable for orchids all the year round, you will perhaps not need a greenhouse. However, you may need some protection against the sun and heavy rain. Lath-houses are ideal for the purpose. A structure is built of 1″ laths spaced about 1″ apart, usually consisting of a roof and three sides only, the fourth side being left open if conditions allow it, facing away from the prevailing wind.

The plants can be grown in pots, boxes or beds, depending on the choice of genera. Care must be taken to make sure that plants do not dry out and remain dry for long periods. It is particularly easy in a large collection to miss plants out when giving them moisture, and so a mist spray controlled by an electronic leaf is advisable in a lath-house.

Many orchids can, if you live in the right parts of, say, Florida or California, be grown in gardens throughout the year. They are usually accommodated on trees or in raised beds of bark compost. Vandas make large plants suitable for hedges, and Oncidiums and Cattleyas look well on trees. More frequent watering will again be necessary than in a greenhouse.

GROWING ORCHIDS INDOORS

If a greenhouse is unavailable and a lath-house is unsuitable, and you do not wish to go to the expense and trouble of an indoor cabinet specially suited for the purpose, it is possible with extra care and attention to grow some orchids in a living-room inside your home. Growing orchids indoors has until quite recently been advised against by the experts, but as so often happens, keen amateurs living in small houses, flats, or apartments have proved them wrong. The essential considerations are still the same—heat, light, air and moisture. It is perhaps best to start with only one or two plants at first, to gain experience, and then add further plants when you are successful.

The room should be capable of maintaining the minimum winter temperature required for the plants chosen; it should face south or south-west to gain as much natural sunlight as possible. A centrally-heated room is obviously best, with a large window unobstructed by curtains. The plants should stand on an inverted flower-pot in a tray or glazed earthenware bowl 3″ deep with a 1″ layer of pebbles and ½″ of water. There will thus be a moist environment round the plants.

If more than one plant is being grown a movable trolley can be used. You can then move it back from the window when the sunlight becomes too direct, and avoid the need for blinds and the like. Pulling it back about 18″ from the window stops the sun from burning the foliage.

The plants must be watched carefully and continuously, as any over-long period of dryness will encourage greenfly and whitefly. It is often a good idea to spray the plants daily with a fine mist. One of the small commercially produced 'atomiser' sprays or a disused scent spray is ideal. Extreme care must be taken that moisture is not allowed to settle in the leaf axils, and all foliage should be dry before nightfall.

Plants benefit if they can be placed outdoors during the summer period *if temperatures allow it*. They should be returned as soon as inclement weather approaches. Do not forget to make sure that the plants are pest-free before you take them in again. A monthly addition of insecticide to the spraying programme is in any case desirable.

Plants which should do well in a room where a minimum temperature of 54°F (12°C) can be maintained include miniature Cymbidiums, Laelia species, Lycaste species, *Dendrobium nobile*, and *D. kingianum, Odontoglossum grande*, Oncidium species, and plain-leaved Paphiopedilums.

Growing orchids indoors is easier and more reliable if you have a suitable container within which to create and control the conditions which orchids like. Back in Victorian times, a plant-collector, named N. B. Ward, invented a glass case for transporting delicate plants on long journeys. Later an adaptation of these could be seen in most Victorian drawing rooms, enclosing delicate plants. These were called 'Wardian cases'. In essence these were airtight glass boxes that kept a moist atmosphere inside. Today, a similar structure, slightly modified and now called a plantarium, is making a comeback and this is ideally suited to the culture of some orchids.

Here you can see what a wide variety of orchids can be grown and flowered together in quite a small greenhouse. There are Dendrobiums and a white Coelogyne (centre), and Epidendrums (top left and centre left); there is a Lycaste (with the beige and yellow flowers, centre), and even a Vanda (centre left).

gravel to allow drainage

Growing orchids on a trolley by the window. It is a good idea not to obstruct the window with curtains. Plenty of light is important, but avoid direct sunlight.

Examples of these simple glass cases suitably equipped with heating, lighting, and fans for air movement are now increasingly seen in hotels, offices and other establishments, containing orchids and other plants.

Home-made versions fitting existing windows, and free-standing versions, are quickly becoming the in-thing. The simplest are of glass or plastic construction in the style of a propagating frame.

A soil cable bedded in sand in the base of the unit for heating, an aquarium strip-light with fluorescent tube for lighting from above, trays of water placed between the plants for humidity, and a movable top for ventilation, provide surroundings suitable for a half-dozen plants or so.

For the real enthusiast larger and more sophisticated cases are available commercially, either free-standing or designed to enclose an existing window. Some are made of transparent acrylic panels, either rectangular or circular in shape, and are very attractive. Others are made of polished aluminium and glass and if arranged with the branches of a tree and suitably furnished with plants they enhance any room.

`Some cases consist of a metal or perspex tray containing drainage material covered with sand, in which is laid a soil cable. Over this is a 2″ layer of peat upon which the plants stand. Others have a metal grill above heating pipes, or can be installed over existing central-heating radiators. Shallow troughs run along both sides, filled with water to give humidity.

Ideal conditions for growing orchids indoors—the plants include Paphio-pedilum, Lycaste, Cattleya, Phalaenopsis, Oncidium, and Dendrobium. Equipment such as this is a great asset, but the amateur must not feel he cannot achieve anything without it.

Heating is controlled by a thermostat and lighting is in the form of fluorescent tubes suspended above the glass top which should be movable to allow for ventilation. Cases that are set into windows may have some sort of blind, either plastic mesh, gauze, or Venetian, to keep out the midday sun.

During winter months the lighting should be kept on for between eight and ten hours each day. Soil cables and heaters range in capacity from 40 to 1,500 watts and allowing for the heat given off by the lights above, do not use very much electricity, especially when controlled by a reliable thermostat.

A large variety of equipment is available—heaters, thermostats, fans, automatic humidifiers, time switches, all of which make for complete automation allowing the plantarium to be left for considerable periods.

A wide range of orchids may be grown in indoor cases, including Cattleya, Lycaste, Odontoglossum, Oncidium, Phalaenopsis, Dendrobium, and Paphiopedilum. Many other plants, such as bromiliads, ferns, rhipsalis, selaginellas, begonias etc, may be added to make a picturesque scene. The orchid-grower does not necessarily have to be a purist.

Plantariums are bringing orchid growing to many people who have not the facilities for a greenhouse, and they make for very economical growing. Whole rooms suitably equipped can be devoted to growing orchids, with plants mounted on tree fern or bark hanging at varying distances from the lights. Some growers have cellars devoted to orchids, grown entirely under artificial lights. Such developments as these show what opportunities there are even for the orchidist without a greenhouse. Orchids are for the apartment-dweller just as much as for the open-air gardener.

OPPOSITE
A stand of wild orchids, Dactilorhiza maculata, *grows within twelve miles of the very centre of London. In an area twenty yards square there are well over 300 plants. Fortunately for their chances of survival, their location is not well known.*

5 Culture and propagation

Orchids can be grown in pots, boxes or wooden baskets; some are grown attached to pieces of tree fern or bark and some in beds of compost, on the floor or made up on benches. Some people, with somewhat bizarre tastes, use the bones of dead animals—sheep skulls, etc—and I have seen *Epidendrum ibaguense* growing in nothing more than an empty upturned bottle half full of sphagnum moss.

Whatever is used to grow orchids in or on, its main purpose is to hold the plant firmly upright and allow water and air to flow freely around it. Ample drainage is important.

CONTAINERS

The choice of containers is largely a personal one, although it depends partly upon the compost being used. Incidentally, 'compost' in the context of orchid-growing means the medium chosen to support the plant, and not soil mixture as with other plants. Clay pots, which are porous, have been used for many years and are ideal even today. Orchid pots used to be made by hand, and they had a rough surface which orchid roots loved to cling to. Indeed, sometimes the only way to release a plant for repotting was to smash the pot. Many pots had holes and slits in the sides that allowed free access to air and atmospheric moisture. Unfortunately today's machine-made pots are quite smooth and without holes—alas, another craft vanishes. Plastics, man-made imitations, are gradually edging clays out, largely for reasons of cost, and they differ from natural clays in their drying-out capacity, and require adjustments in the watering programme. If you have pots of both types, clay and plastic, in your collection, this can lead to over-watering of the plants in plastic containers, if you are not careful, and is to be avoided. Some thin-walled plastic pots tend to become very brittle because of the action of sunlight, so much so that the mere lifting of a pot by the rim can cause it to shatter, leaving you with a small piece of the pot in your hand, and the smashed or mutilated plant on the floor. The thicker, soft, rubbery type of plastic

OPPOSITE
Here, tropical plants, ferns and bromiliads are brought in to complement the orchids, which include Paphiopedilum and Oncidium.

pot is longer-lasting and a safer buy. Square-shaped pots tend to make for a more efficient use of space as they can be placed side-by-side, close together. This arrangement also seems to allow for the more even evaporation of moisture, but it can lead to overcrowding and unless due care is taken the compost can become waterlogged, with fatal consequences for the plants.

Teak, oak, and cedar slatted baskets are useful for many orchids, indeed they are essential for plants like Stanhopeas where flower stems hang downwards from the base of the plant. These plants were grown for many years in pots in the past, and never flowered. Then, one day, a plant was dropped in a nursery when it was being re-potted by an observant grower, and the flower stem and buds were seen among the roots of the plant, where every year they had tried to push their way through the bottom of the pot. Unable to get through they had just rotted away. These plants are now always grown in baskets and flower regularly. Baskets are now available also in plastic.

Many orchids, mainly terrestrial types, are grown in beds of specially prepared compost on the floors of larger greenhouses. Many Cymbidiums, in particular, are grown commercially by this method, which allows more plants to the square yard and reduces the labour of re-potting. Very large plants can be produced in this way, with as many as twenty flower spikes on each. The amateur, unable to spare the space, and usually growing other plants with his Cymbidiums, does the next-best thing by planting in 18″ or 2′ square teak or cedar boxes about 6″ deep. This allows for the vigorous root system the plant produces. Alternatively a much larger box, say 8′ × 3′ × 6″, can be made up on the greenhouse bench.

Many epiphytic orchids grow particularly well on slabs, rafts, blocks or poles of tree fern. The plants are tied in position, usually with a pad of sphagnum moss underneath, with either thin wire or nylon and very soon root into the tree fern. This is the nearest method to nature one can get. Very often pieces of cork bark are used, and if you have enough to make into a small tree it can be very attractive.

COMPOSTS

The first orchids imported both into Europe and North America were grown in a variety of peat mixtures. Leaf mould was tried too, but neither peat mixture nor leaf mould was very successful, as both were too easily waterlogged. With the introduction of osmunda fibre and moss mixture, orchids rapidly flourished and for many years this was the only recognised compost. The origin of the use of this has always intrigued people— it is the root of the *Osmunda regalis* fern, sifted to remove the dust, and hand-picked to remove any impurities. The black wiry root is cut into pieces about 2″ long, then gathered into small bunches and, with the fibres upright, packed very tightly around the roots of the orchid, until the plant is securely held. It was often said that if you smashed every other pot when re-potting, your plants were correctly potted. Plants in osmunda were never fed with fertilisers, as the fibres themselves contain nitrogen, phosphate and potassium, as well as other trace elements.

The addition of about one-third live sphagnum moss with a sprinkling of charcoal kept the compost moist and sweet. The heads of the live sphagnum moss were used in the topmost layer and when plants were

Coelogyne cristata is a cool-growing plant, and a rewarding one for the beginner to try, with its beautiful sprays of crystal-white 3" flowers.

watered correctly with rain-water, the moss grew with a nice, rich, green colour. This gave the grower an insight into his plant's watering needs, for if a plant was dry the moss would appear whiteish.

With the introduction of mains water, due to the addition of certain purifying agents which altered the pH (the accepted measure of acidity or alkalinity) of the water, the moss did not react like this. This has given rise to the old saying, 'Orchids must be watered with rain-water'. Orchid plants resent a compost or water that is too acid or too alkaline. They need a slightly acid condition, pH6, which is just under halfway along the pH scale nought to fourteen.

Osmunda fern grows wild in various parts of the world but the best comes from Japan. But as often happens when Man uses a natural commodity, it became scarce and the price increased. What with the effects of war and the spread of the concrete jungle today, osmunda is far too expensive to buy. So alternatives have been tried by enthusiastic amateurs: peat, charcoal, dried leaves, coke, plastic, tree fern, cork, moss, polystyrene, bark and vermiculite—all have been tried either singly or as mixtures; they have had degrees of success and all have their followers.

Stanhopeas growing in slatted baskets hanging in the greenhouse. The flower stems hang downwards from the base of the plant.

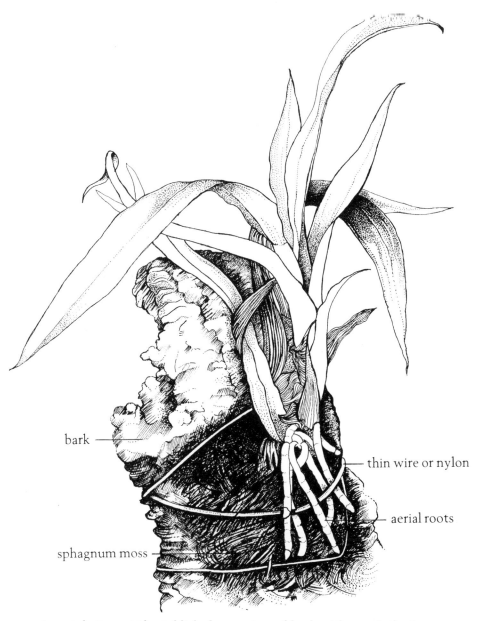

bark

thin wire or nylon

aerial roots

sphagnum moss

An epiphytic orchid established on a piece of bark with a pad of sphagnum moss.

The most widely used have been bark; hard lumpy peat; and sphagnum peat and plastic mixture, this last mainly on the continent of Europe. Fibrous moss peat, mixed with an equal quantity of plastic or polystyrene chips, does tend to waterlog in inexperienced hands. Hard peat in approximately $\frac{1}{2}''$ pieces mixed equally with redwood chips is excellent for the larger-rooted plants.

The most popular composts for all types of orchids at the moment are the various bark mixes. The capacity of the compost to retain moisture is controlled by the amount of live sphagnum moss in it.

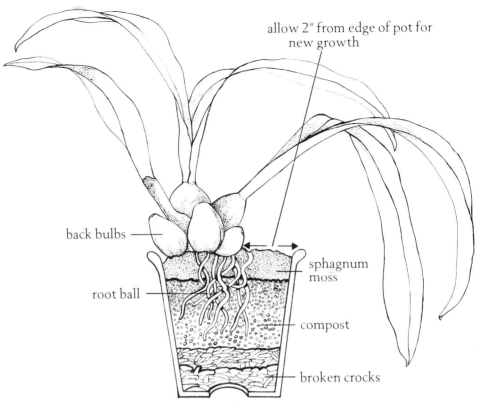

allow 2″ from edge of pot for
new growth

back bulbs

root ball

sphagnum
moss

compost

broken crocks

Correct potting of a terrestrial orchid.

The bark from certain species of conifers, shredded or chopped into suitable sizes, is used either alone or mixed with live sphagnum moss, perlite or polystyrene. It is readily available from most orchid nurseries, and many versions are commercially produced under various trade names in the USA.

Most barks are today cleaned by the suppliers, and available in pieces of about four different sizes. All need the regular addition of fertiliser, especially nitrogen. Most nurseries have their own formula for fertilisers, and they are freely advertised in the various orchid journals.

One point to remember when using bark is that it invariably arrives in a dry state, having lost its hygroscopic ability (the ability to absorb moisture). Ordinary water will not dampen it, so add a few drops of a proprietary wetting agent or washing-up liquid to the water. Many plants have shrivelled up and died for the lack of this precaution.

POTTING

Potting in today's compost is comparatively simple. First, shake off all the existing compost from the roots of the plant. Then place a layer of broken crocks or small pieces of polystyrene in the bottom of the pot for drainage; place enough bark compost under the plant so that it sits comfortably with the base of the bulbs or rhizome level with the top of the pot. Allow enough room for two or more growths to develop forward then gently fill the pot with the compost until it is level with the bulbs, gently firming down the surface with the thumbs all the time. Finish off by clipping on a clipstake or rhizome clip, or insert a cane and tie the plant securely, then place the plant in a humid, shady part of the greenhouse for a week or so.

WATERING

Watering orchids is the most difficult part of growing for the beginner to grasp. When does wet become too wet and how dry is dry? The mere fact of worrying over it causes many to err on the wrong side. Orchids in natural conditions are soaked with rain, but quickly dry out at the root when the sun shines. Water collects in the leaf axil but, again, with the action of wind and sun it rapidly evaporates. Most orchids have pseudo-bulbs that enable them to store water, so they can go a considerable period without rain, the roots taking moisture from the humidity around them.

In cultivation we must try to emulate this process by giving the plants a good soaking, then allowing the compost to dry out. The frequency of the treatment depends upon the weather conditions at the time. A well-tried maxim for beginners is, if you think a plant needs water leave it until the next day. If a plant has been correctly potted in an open compost, water should drain away almost immediately but if it has been rammed in too hard the compost will remain wet and soggy inside, even though the top is dry, with disastrous results. Unfortunately orchids, being slow-growing plants, show no signs of distress until some time after the event

On the roots of an epiphytic orchid is a membraneous sheath, the 'velamen'. When the plant is resting, the velamen extends to the end of the roots, and there is no green tip. This gives an indication of the watering and feeding requirements.

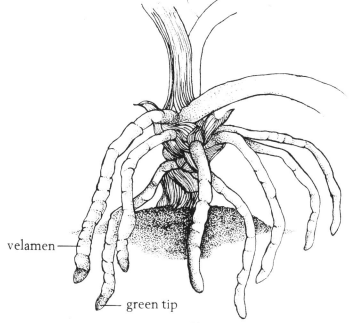

velamen

green tip

which caused it. The leaves turn yellow and fall off, the pseudobulbs shrivel and the plant dies. Unfortunately the symptoms are much the same whether the plant is too wet or too dry.

Any plant is only as good as its roots and these are always a good indicator of a plant's state of health. Frequent inspection of a plant's roots will guide you—if they are soft, brown or black the compost is too wet. Roots should be hard, firm and white-looking, with a brown or green tip.

Watering will only be mastered with experience. Orchids should be watered in the mornings so that moisture on the foliage has time to dry before nightfall. Any water lying in the leaf axils should be removed with a piece of tissue or cotton-wool, otherwise rot will soon set in. It is preferable to use rainwater due to its softness, but mains water is perfectly acceptable and the hardness can be controlled by the addition of a softener. If plants look sickly it is advisable to have your mains water tested. Water should always be of approximately the same temperature as the greenhouse—a sudden soaking with cold water is not advisable. Those fortunate enough to live where the temperature allows plants to be grown in a lath-house will find their plants dry-out fairly quickly and will need water more regularly. The same applies to plants grown in beds in tropical areas.

ATMOSPHERIC MOISTURE

The percentage of atmospheric moisture, or humidity, is most important to orchids. Minute particles of water are suspended in the air, and this water is taken up by the plants' roots and leaves. The amount of moisture varies with different climates and with different greenhouses. Some are naturally moist, others very dry. The humidity level is measured on an instrument called a hygrometer and a reading of between 70 and 80% should be aimed for.

In natural conditions 'relative humidity' varies inversely with the temperature: when the temperature rises, relative humidity falls, when the temperature falls, relative humidity rises. So it must be remembered that as the temperature rises in our greenhouse, so the humidity reading falls, but towards evening when the temperature falls the humidity reading rises; and if the greenhouse is too wet, this humidity will be deposited as condensation on the glass which can form into drips and these will harm our plants. So we must damp down early in the day to allow the house to become dryer before evening.

Damping down is done by spraying water onto the floors and benches, or by an automatic misting apparatus controlled by an electronic leaf, which switches it on when a certain degree of dryness is obtained. During winter, trays of water placed above the heater will create the desired results but care must be taken to see it is not overdone; otherwise wet rot and fungus disease will follow. Many greenhouses have ferns, mosses and other foliage plants growing under the benches—these also help to maintain a moist atmosphere.

If the greenhouse is lined with polythene this helps to retain the humidity, as well as insulate against heat loss. With sufficient humidity in the air, less water is required in the pots or containers, as the compost will take longer to dry out. If you find your plants are drying out almost daily, step up your humidity until a correct balance is achieved. But remember during winter a big drop in the temperature must be avoided.

FEEDING

All living things need food and orchids are no exception. Alas, many plants died in the early days of orchid-growing through the use of the wrong fertilisers; but latter-day research has proved orchids can benefit if fertilisers are correctly given. Supplies of nitrogen, phosphates and potassium are essential to the well-being of all plants. Nitrogen promotes healthy stems and foliage, phosphates are given for correct development of roots and flowers and resistance to disease. Complete fertilisers are sold under various trade-names and are invariably recognised by the proportions they contain of these three constituents, expressed always in the same order. For example 30–10–10, or 30N–10P–10K, contains a high proportion of nitrogen for good growth; 10–30–20, or 10N–30P–20K, contains a high proportion of phosphates and potassium for good flower-production. Many variations are available commercially.

It must be borne in mind that only good, strong, healthy plants can assimilate extra food and also that conditions must be right when you give fertilisers. It is no good giving extra nitrogen in poor, winter-light conditions—you will only end up with long, weak, sappy growths and no flowers.

Good light is necessary for good growth and fertiliser can be given then; but remember, too strong a mixture will kill your roots. It is far better to give a weak solution regularly than an occasional strong one. A soaking of clear water after each third feed is advisable to avoid a build-up of salts in the compost. A sign of this is the root tips dying when they reach the sides of the pot.

LIGHT AND SHADING

Orchids need good light for photosynthesis. In nature they can take the full power of the sun without being burnt—this is because there is usually a cool, moist breeze blowing at the same time. Amateurs' green-houses are usually heavily shaded to try and keep the temperature within reasonable limits. The need for shading can be reduced if you have a fan running under the staging to keep the air moving. This reduces the risk of scorching the leaves. A simple test of the light is to hold your hand above the plant; if it throws a faint shadow, the light is about right.

The best type of shading is a slatted blind, made of timber or plastic, that can be rolled up or down. If it can be controlled automatically by a photo-sensitive cell, so much the better. Although this adds to one's expense it is well worth the cost. Roller blinds of plastic mesh are a worthwhile alternative. These should normally be positioned about 3" above the glass, leaving an air space that acts as an insulator. All these devices help to keep a more equable temperature in the orchid-house.

Permanent shading in the form of whitening can be applied to the glass (proprietary brands are available) but it does restrict essential light on dull days. The quantity of shading required will increase or decrease according to the latitude at which the greenhouse is located. But remember *light* is important: we only shade to keep the *temperature* down, or to prevent foliage from being burnt by over-strong, direct sunlight. Shading should be ready in early spring to protect the plants from the first bursts of sunshine. Plants are at that time most susceptible after the sunless winter, and during early autumn (fall) shading should be reduced gradually.

VENTILATION

Fresh air is vital to orchids as it supplies them with carbon dioxide, as well as keeping the atmosphere buoyant, but fresh air does not mean cold icy blasts; under-staging ventilators should be open slightly at all times to allow a current of air to circulate. There should be only a chink of top ventilation, otherwise all the precious moisture will disappear out of the top of the orchid-house, leaving the atmosphere too dry.

PROPAGATION

Once plants have been grown successfully for a year or so, you will probably begin to think of increasing your stock; maybe you would like to have two examples of one plant, or pass a piece on to a friend. What do you do?

Orchids are increased by division, in one form or another, or by seed. The latter is, I feel, a technique beyond the scope of this book, which is intended mainly for the beginner. It is unwise for the inexperienced grower purposely to fertilise his plant to obtain seed until he has mastered the growing of good, strong, healthy plants capable of taking the strain of carrying seed-pods. Other books are available which go into such methods of propagation in more detail, and are listed later.

Division of an orchid plant can be effected firstly by cutting the plant in two; secondly by taking a small plant such as sometimes appears on an old pseudobulb or flower-stem, and which is called a 'ki-ki'; or thirdly by a laboratory technique called meristem culture. This last will not concern the amateur orchid-lover.

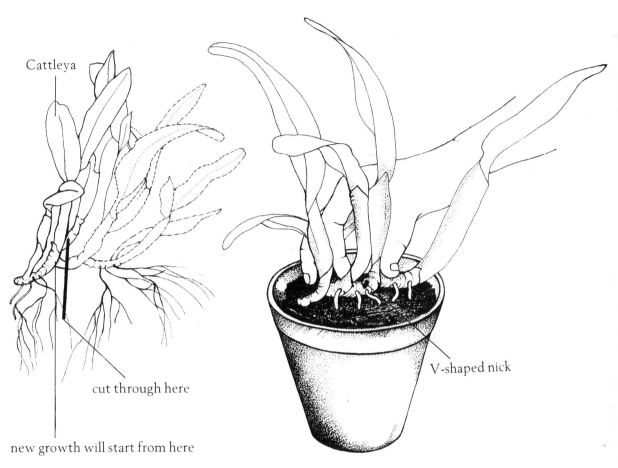

Cattleya

cut through here

new growth will start from here

V-shaped nick

Propagating a Cattleya. In the right-hand drawing the V-shaped nick can be seen in the rhizome, which over the winter will cause new growth to appear. If the cut is completed in the spring, and continued down through the compost, the propagation can be potted up with the minimum of disturbance.

One method of propagation is specially applicable to plants which have pseudobulbs, such as Cattleyas, Odontoglossums, Miltonias, and Cymbidiums. If you have a plant with say six or more pseudobulbs, the rhizome can be severed behind the fourth, giving you two pieces: one with four bulbs and one with two. The latter piece is called a 'back-bulb propagation'; when separated from the parent piece it is usually found to contain only one or two live roots and often none at all. If these pseudobulbs are placed into plastic bags containing an inch or so of moist, live sphagnum moss and hung in a shady spot, in a few months new roots should develop and latent eyes at the base of the pseudobulbs show signs

This top cutting of a Dendrobium is ready to be inserted into compost, and placed into a propagator or plastic bag until roots form.

of life. When roots and growth are about 3″ high, they are potted into the normal compost and, given extra care, grow into another plant. Division can be done while the plant is still in the pot and in some respects this is advisable for the amateur making his first couple of attempts. Instead of cutting right through the rhizome and separating right away, a V-shaped nick is made in the autumn (fall) half-way through the rhizome, and the plant left until the spring; then it will be found that the latent eye has grown and new roots put into the existing compost. When repotting, with a sharp knife continue the cut right through the rhizome and the compost. You will then have a growing plant ready that can be carefully potted up without too much disturbance.

It must be stressed that at least two pseudobulbs should be left on each back-propagation. The method of nicking the rhizome may also be used to increase the number of growths on such plants as Cattleyas—if the rhizome is nicked to encourage dormant eyes to grow, a single-growthed plant will soon develop multiple growths and produce extra flowers.

Some orchids, principally Dendrobiums and Epidendrums, produce new plants at the tops, ends or sides of their stems; these are called 'adventitious' growths. When their roots are about 2″ long they should be carefully separated and potted up. Some Phalaenopsis will produce small plantlets on the ends of the flower spikes: these are treated likewise.

Dendrobiums may be also increased by removing one or two sound, leafless pseudobulbs and cutting them just below a node into pieces 3–6″ long. These are then stood upright in well-drained trays or pots of chopped-up, live sphagnum moss and, if placed in a warm, moist propagator, they will soon produce roots and growths. Single, sound, leafless Cymbidium and Odontoglossum back-bulbs may also be propagated in this manner.

Paphiopedilums and Masdevallias should be divided only when sufficiently large, with multiple growths. When they are being repotted in the summer, plants should be carefully prised apart in pieces of at least four growths each, taking care not to break the roots; often when repotting these pieces will be found to be already separated.

Vandas and related plants often produce side-shoots; these should be allowed to develop roots of about 3″. Then carefully detach them by slicing with a sharp knife. Do remember to sterilise any cutting instrument before each individual incision. Sometimes Vandas and related plants grow into tall, leggy specimens. Provided the top has some roots attached to it, it may be cut off and potted up; the bottom section will very often produce new side-shoots; if the top of the plant is devoid of roots, these may be encouraged by wrapping moist sphagnum moss around the bare stem below the leaves. When new roots are about 4″ long, the top may be cut off.

It is pointless to propagate plants just for fun. Not only do propagations take a considerable time to grow into flowering-size plants, but a greenhouse full of many small plants cannot compare with a lesser number of large, multi-growthed, many-flowered specimens. So, unless you have a particularly fine plant, and you feel that a spare is necessary in case of any unforeseen mishaps, do try and grow large, specimen plants. 'Cultural awards' are granted by orchid societies all over the world. One grows orchids for their own sake as much as for the winning of awards; but all the same, it is well worth striving for plants you can be proud of.

6 Pests and diseases

Most writers on growing plants do their best to encourage the reader, but then finish up with a horror chapter enough to dampen the spirits of the most ardent enthusiast. Grossly magnified drawings of insects, lurid descriptions of diseases, together with a list of highly poisonous substances, so terrify the prospective grower that he cannot enter his own greenhouse without thoughts of attack by voracious insects, or sudden death caused by the lingering residue of poisonous chemicals.

Let us not get pests and diseases out of proportion. Of course all plants are subject to attacks by pests and disease. So is man, but that does not mean we all walk around looking like drugstores; we have learnt that with proper food, care and cleanliness, many attacks can be avoided. So it can be with our plants.

Nearly all plants purchased from reputable orchid nurseries are clean and healthy. Even so, the most thorough inspection should be given before placing a new plant in the home or greenhouse. The main cause of trouble is plants acquired from well-meaning friends. These can bring with them a multitude of difficulties. They can contaminate a whole collection in a matter of days, and it can take months to eradicate the problem. No plant should be placed in your collection without first being immersed, pot and all, in a bucket of insecticide. Any specific pest you have noticed should be given individual treatment. This will save hours of work which could be necessary later if the thing is allowed to develop.

Unfortunately conditions suitable for orchids are ideal also for the prolific breeding of our foes, so it is important to make every endeavour to keep them out. Even though they are fairly tough, plants will soon succumb and weaken, taking a long time to recover, if seriously attacked by such pests as aphids, mealy-bug, red spider, scale, slugs, or thrips; or if certain diseases are allowed to develop by bad culture. On the principle that 'prevention is better than cure', let us look at some simple precautions we can take as a first line of defence.

OPPOSITE

The beautiful, rose-purple flowers of Cattleya bowringiana *grow on tall spikes, up to twenty on each.*

If we take care not to introduce pests on plants ourselves, where do they come from and how do they get in? As pests are mainly flying or crawling creatures, openings such as ventilators, and cracks around the bottom of structures must be suspect. So be sure to fill all cracks around the bases of greenhouses; ventilators should be covered with fine mesh-like plastic, or gauze. A separate, hinged door-frame covered with the same material will cut down the entry of the larger creatures and at least help to deter the smaller. Garden plants should not be grown within 3' of the greenhouse walls and any weeds appearing there should be scrupulously destroyed. Insects naturally lay their eggs in a place safe from other predatory animals and within reach of suitable food. Our object is to make sure they go in the opposite direction to the greenhouse.

A dressing of lime scattered around the outside wall will deter those voracious feeders, the slug and the snail, and a scattering of proprietary metaldehyde-based slug pellets inside should take care of any that get through. These must be replaced after rain.

Ants will make their way into the greenhouse and make their nest in the compost in the pots. They are very effective as 'Estate Agents' carrying other pests such as aphis and scale from one plant to another and so throughout the greenhouse. Fortunately ants are very much creatures of habit and invariably all use the same path or trail, so they are easily detected. Control should be effected with one of the commercially produced ant-killers, which, when eaten by the ant, create a virus that swiftly spreads and kills the whole nest.

Having done our best to deter as many pests as possible how do we control those that do get past our defences? Many new chemical compounds are proving effective in the control of pests, but alas many side- and after-effects are coming to light. Other creatures, even man himself, can be affected, for example by DDT and chlorocide. I am reluctant to advise the use of these new chemical preparations even if extreme care is taken. Other more natural, less lethal methods seem preferable, anyone wishing to use the more modern, perhaps speedier methods had best consult his orchid nurseryman or the current literature on the subject.

If we have taken proper care and precautions very few of the pests listed below will appear in our houses, and if they do, numbers should be very small indeed.

Thrips are very small greyish-brown winged insects of minute dimensions that attack the leaves, shoots, flowers and roots of orchids, causing minute rusty spotting on the leaves and twisting of the buds and shoots by means of sucking of the sap. They should be controlled with strong, soapy water or a nicotine spray, administered every five days until the plants are clear.

Mealy-bug, or *Woolly aphis*, looks, as the latter name implies, like small, downy cotton-wool masses that congregate under the protective bracts on pseudobulbs, on stems, and underneath the leaves. The scale-like insect covers itself with this white, protective covering. Mealy-bugs are prolific breeders, each female laying 500 or more eggs every twenty-one days. If ants are active on the plant check for this pest, which produces a honey-like substance that ants enjoy. Black sooty marks on leaves also indicate the presence of mealy-bug; control them by dipping a small paint-brush in methylated spirit and regularly dab each infestation until it has cleared.

Scale is a tenacious, sucking insect. At first glance they look dead, like small blisters about 1/6″ long on the underneath of the leaves, around the stems and bottoms of pseudobulbs. Control by painting with methylated spirits, as for mealy-bug. The marks left by the insect will unfortunately remain. Continued weekly application is indicated until the plant is clear. Then spray with soapy water.

Red spider mites are minute, and are generally not noticed until a large colony has built up. They are usually associated with too-dry conditions. The foliage takes on a silvery appearance due to the sap being sucked out, and upon close examination minute red or yellow, peppery-looking dots are seen; these are the mites, and are sometimes covered by very fine webs. Red spider mites are very prolific breeders; about a hundred eggs laid by each mite every fourteen days can soon ruin a collection of the softer-leafed orchids. Dendrobiums, Miltonias and Odontoglossum are favourite victims. Control is difficult. Strong soapy water is used if the attack is seen earlier; otherwise one of the newer proprietary insecticides or smoke bombs must be resorted to. Again, marks on leaves remain. A fresh, moist atmosphere is the best deterrent.

Slugs and Snails, voracious feeders, will eat your choice blooms or shoots overnight if allowed entry. They are best controlled as soon as the tell-tale silvery trail is seen: wait until dark, then, with a torch or flashlight, go to the infected plant and when found despatch the culprit with the heel of your boot. One or two maidenhair ferns (*Adiantum cuneatum*) placed among your orchids, besides looking decorative, will attract any snails or slugs in preference to your orchid. It is amazing how the intruders find them. Proprietary brands of slug-killer in liquid form should be watered over your orchids and benches every six weeks.

Aphids (greenfly or plant lice) usually infest the unopened buds and stems, causing distortion of flowers and buds. Strong soapy water or a nicotine-based spray will soon deal with these.

All the above pests pierce the plants tissue and can cause virus infections. Constant vigilance, good healthy plants, and scrupulous cleanliness are the best defences.

DISEASES

Diseases, too, are most often caused by bad growing conditions and are mainly of fungus type—black rot, leaf spot and soft rot—and are encouraged by low temperatures with high humidity. A proper relationship between temperature, humidity and the amount of fresh air should prevent them.

Strong, well-grown, pest-free plants are seldom sufferers of disease. Constant careful handling of your plants will soon bring to light any strange symptoms, so that immediate action can be taken to establish the cause. As orchids are slow-growing plants, it is often some considerable time after the cause before distress is shown. Constant observation must therefore be the rule. A period of incorrect watering—either too much or too little—will make itself known by yellowing and dropping of the leaves; but, alas, not until perhaps eight weeks later. By this time the

A well-flowered example of Leptotes bicolor—*if your plants are strong and well-grown, and kept free of pests, they are less likely to suffer from disease.*

plant has lost all its roots. Either it will die, or at least many months of careful culture will be required before the plant recovers to its former state.

Diseases are usually of a bacterial or fungal nature, and are caused by too-damp, close conditions, or by a combination of low temperatures with high humidity. Black or brown spots and blemishes appear on the bulbs, roots or flowers; these quickly develop into soft rotting tissue that quickly spreads. A complete plant can die in less than a week.

Prompt action, by removing the affected part cutting right back into clean tissue with a sterilised knife and dusting the cut with sulphur powder or powdered charcoal, should check the rot. A thorough check on all other plants in the near vicinity should then be made. Any showing signs should be dealt with immediately.

A number of fungicides are available from orchid nurseries, who should be consulted if the outbreak is severe. Proper balanced control of heating, humidity and ventilation, no sudden drops in temperature whilst humidity is high, no debris such as old leaves left to become breeding places for fungus—these are the aims. Any bare tissue exposed when, for example, flowers are cut, should be dusted with sulphur to prevent the entry of fungus spores. Any knives or blades should be sterilised by being passed through a flame before and during use on each occasion.

Remember, strong, healthy plants are least likely to be attacked; prevention is better than cure.

The worst disease encountered in growing orchids is virus. Fortunately not all that common, it appears in various forms, such as light spots and streaks that, when viewed against the light, appear transparent. Later they turn into black streaky masses, and cause distorted and stunted growths and flowers. Brownish purple-pitted spots are one symptom, and eventually merge into larger areas.

Unfortunately virus is difficult to identify positively without the aid of a trained virologist. Your orchid nurseryman will help you here. As virus diseases live in the cells of a plant, there is no known cure. Any propagation or part of the plant will carry the infection. Unless of outstanding value, infected plants should be burnt.

Viruses are microscopic living organisms, which can reproduce only in the environment of a specific plant's cell; they invade the cell breaking it down to reproduce more of their own insidious selves, gradually killing the plant. They can only attack a healthy plant through wounds or the like; therefore virus can only be transmitted if insects pierce the plant or man cuts it. The only defence is, again, control of pests and absolute cleanliness of all cutting tools.

7 What do the names mean?

If you are new to horticulture and you are confronted with a name like *Phalaenopsis lueddemanniana var. hieroglyphica 'Olga'*, you may well be perplexed, and feel you will never know what the experts are talking about. But don't give up hope. With explanations and familiarity one soon masters the names.

Latin is used for all plant names. It may seem complicated but it has the great advantage of being accepted and universally understood. All plants belong to a 'natural order': this book is about the Orchidaceae: all plants in that natural order are called 'orchids'.

The group is split into sub-divisions that contain plants with certain similar botanical characteristics; this sub-division carries the generic name, that of the 'genus' to which the particular plant belongs. It should always be written starting with a capital letter, e.g. *Phalaenopsis*.

Each genus is divided into species, and so next comes the specific name, that of the species. It should always be written with a small letter, e.g. *Phalaenopsis lueddemanniana*. The specific names are a great help in that they usually describe some feature of the plant. For example, 'flavus' means yellow, 'gracilis' graceful, 'incurvum' bent, and so on. These are given in the Glossary at the end of the book.

Next comes the variety name. Like the specific name, the variety name should have a small letter, but it is preceded by the word *'var'*. The variety name indicates that the plant has some distinguishing feature not found in the species in general—for example *Phalaenopsis lueddemanniana var. hieroglyphica*.

Next may come a name given by the grower to his particular plant, usually when it has some outstanding feature or has won an award. This is known as the cultivar name, and should always be enclosed in single quotation marks. And so we end up with *Phalaenopsis lueddemanniana var. hieroglyphica 'Olga'*. Where a name includes a cultivar name, it can only be applied to the particular plant it was first given to, or to vegetative divisions of it.

Sometimes letters follow the cultivar name; these signify awards that have been won. Examples are /FCC (First Class Certificate) or JC (Judges' Commendation). Following that may be more initials, denoting the society that gave the award—for example /JC/CSA (Cymbidium Society of America) or /FCC/RHS (Royal Horticultural Society). There is a list of such initials in the Glossary at the end of the book.

When two species of the same name are crossed, the resulting plants carry the same specific name; but if two *different* species are crossed, the resulting seedlings are called 'hybrids', and are given a different name.

Orchids differ from other plants in that different genera readily interbreed. The opportunities for the enterprising grower are therefore almost limitless, and Man is continuously trying to produce flowers better in all kinds of ways than Mother Nature herself. For these hybrids new generic names are created, generally by combining the names of the genera used in the cross. For example, Laelicattleya is a cross between Laelia and Cattleya; Aeridopsis is a cross between Aerides and Phalaenopsis.

Orchids interbreed so freely that sometimes three or four genera are used in one cross. For the resulting new genus a name has to be formed, and this must end in '-ara'. So we get names like Potinara (Brassavola × Cattleya × Laelia × Sophronitis) or Vuylstekeara (Odontoglossum × Cochlioda × Miltonia).

A complete list of these names and parents can be found in *The Handbook on Orchid Nomenclature and Registration*, obtainable from the American Orchid Society, or the Royal Horticultural Society in England.

Ever since the first hybrid was flowered by the firm of J. Veitch and Sons in October 1856, a register of crosses has been kept by the famous English orchid family of Sander. The orchid world must be eternally grateful to them, for this register enables one to trace the parentage and progeny of practically every named orchid.

This, with the painting of every award-winning plant kept by the Royal Horticultural Society, has done much to enable breeders to obtain the successes of the past decade.

In the continual attempts to obtain larger, rounder and more colourful flowers, and robuster plants, great improvements have taken place. Millions of failures have occurred—Nature does not let Man have it all his own way, but the successes have to be seen to be appreciated.

Many orchid-growers prefer to grow only natural species; they abhor the large man-made flowers. Certainly for grace and beauty the natural species are difficult to beat, but nevertheless wonderful flowers have been produced by Man. This is a matter of personal choice. I have never seen an ugly orchid.

8 Some orchids to grow

The orchids described in this chapter obviously cover only a fraction of the complete range. They have been chosen because in my experience they are easily grown by the beginner. No doubt some orchidists will disagree with my selection, having perhaps had difficulty with some of them themselves. I too have had my failures, but on the whole you should be successful with many of them.

Beginners do not generally want to pay vast sums when buying plants. This is why most of the descriptions on the following pages are of orchid species, rather than the hybrids which you will often see at shows. The simple species are usually cheaper and more easily available, and can be grown into marvellous, specimen plants.

Aerangis

Kenya and Madagascar

The Aerangis orchids are epiphytic plants. The flowers are white or yellow in colour, star-shaped with a distinct spur. An Aerangis will tolerate temperatures down to about 60°F (16°C), and will benefit from daily syringing during the summer months. It should not be allowed to dry out completely, but needs relatively little light.

Aerangis will grow on pieces of bark or tree fern, or attached to the branches of a tree, and is very suitable for inclusion in an indoor plantarium. It will flower over six to eight weeks in the period from November to April. Most Aerangis are not highly scented.

SPECIES

A. citrata has fleshy leaves, some 4″ long and 1″ wide. The blooms stem from the base of the plant in racemes 10–15″ long, carrying up to fifteen pale-yellow star-shaped flowers 1″ in diameter and with a spur $1\frac{1}{2}$″ long. This spring-flowering species comes from Madagascar.

OPPOSITE

Oncidium papilio *can be a challenge to the grower and is not easy to flower, but the flowers, 3–4″ across, are very long-lasting—some last two months. It is known as the 'butterfly orchid', because of its appearance.*

A. rhodosticta has a very short, almost non-existent plant stem, and fleshy leaves 3″ long. There are usually ten or more flowers 1″ in diameter on stems 12″ long, originating at the base of the plant. This is a delightful orchid, flowering around March and April. The blooms are flat, creamy-white with orange-red centres. *A. rhodosticta* comes originally from Kenya.

Anguloa
Columbia and Peru

The Anguloa is commonly known as the 'tulip' or 'cradle' orchid. This is because the lip is hinged, and rocks backwards and forwards.

This is an epiphytic orchid: in the natural state it is found growing on mossy rocks and branches high in the Andes, in South America. The 2–3″-long pseudobulbs carry from two to four 24″-long, broad, plicate leaves very erect, while the single tulip-shaped flowers are thick and fleshy, and generally golden-yellow in colour. Several stems 8–10″ long rise from the base of the pseudobulbs of the previous year, usually carrying the new growths in late spring or early summer. The Anguloa is very heavily scented, flowering for four to five weeks in the period March to May.

The Anguloa needs moist, shady conditions, with a minimum temperature of 52–60°F (11–16°C), according to the species. The plant should be rested, in dry conditions, from October to December. It is a large plant—Anguloas require a fair amount of room.

Anguloa has been crossed with Lycaste to produce Angulocaste.

SPECIES

A. cliftonii bears flowers of a golden-yellow colour, reddish-brown at the base. It comes from Peru, and needs a minimum temperature of 60°F (15°C).

A. clowesii has rich golden-yellow, cup-shaped flowers with a whiteish lip. It comes originally from Colombia, and is notable for its fragrance. It will survive temperatures down to 52°F (11°C).

Ansellia
East and West Africa

Ansellia was named after the nineteenth-century botanist, John Ansell. Because of its yellow colour and brown markings, it is commonly called the 'leopard orchid'.

This is a scented, epiphytic orchid, 12–48″ high, with long, thin pseudobulbs and numerous lanceolate leaves. Another distinctive feature is the erect, 2′-long terminal panicle of lovely flowers, 1–1½″ in diameter. These bloom several times a year, usually during the autumn (fall) and winter, although flowers can appear at other times.

Ansellia should be hung or stood in a light position. Watering should be thorough, but the plant should be allowed to dry out well afterwards. It likes a minimum night temperature of 60°F (16°C). After the plant has flowered, it should be rested for six weeks.

Ansellia has been crossed with Cymbidium to give Ansidium.

SPECIES

A. africana has yellow flowers 1″ in diameter with purple-brown cross markings. The pseudobulbs are 2″ long.

A. gigantea has pale-yellow flowers 1½″ in diameter, with brownish markings—these are very variable in colour, usually a nigger-brown, but sometimes anything from a darker yellow to almost black. The pseudobulbs are 3–4″ long.

Brassavola

Central America

Named after a Venetian botanist, Dr Angelo Brassavolo, this epiphytic genus is renowned for its ability to impart its huge frilly lip to other genera with which it is hybridised. The species *digbyana*, described more fully below, has been used particularly widely.

The different Brassavola species vary enormously in their appearance, and it is almost impossible to give a general description. The flowers range from 1″ to 5″ in diameter; they are usually star-shaped, and vary in colour from white to yellow, often with brownish markings. Leaves are usually terete in form, from 4″ to 18″ in length. The lip is the most characteristic feature, usually very frilly.

Brassavolas need much the same conditions as Cattleyas, described elsewhere; give them a piece of bark, or tree fern, in a fairly light and moist position, with regular watering.

SPECIES

B. cucullata, known as the 'Ghost Orchid', because of its ethereal appearance, has long, stem-like pseudobulbs with thin, terete leaves 20″ long, with two or more white, fragrant flowers that appear from the top of the pseudobulbs. The flowers have starry petals, 4″ across and a beautiful heart-shaped white lip. This fragrant species likes particularly to grow on a piece of bark, or hanging in a basket. It comes from Mexico. Minimum growing temperature 55°F (13°C). *B. nodosa* is similar in appearance.

B. digbyana has now been reclassified as *Rhyncholaelia digbyana* but is listed here under its old name, for this is the name under which it has become famous owing to its usefulness in breeding. It has club-shaped pseudobulbs about 6″ high with a solitary thick, fleshy, bluish-green leaf. In the summer it produces a single flower which lasts about five weeks, 5″ across, with whitish-green, narrow petals and a very large creamy-white lip which is beautifully fringed.

When this species is used in crossing, the frilly lip is generally reflected in the progeny—*B. digbyana* is responsible for the beautiful, frilled lips on such hybrids as Brassocattleya and Brassolaeliocattleya. This species which comes from Mexico, should be rested for six weeks. It will survive temperatures down to 60°F (16°C), and therefore needs warmer conditions than the true Brassavolas. It comes from Costa Rica.

B. glauca, like *B. digbyana*, has been transferred to the genus *Rhyncholaelia*; indeed it is very similar to *B. digbyana* except that it lacks the fringe on the lip. The whole plant is also smaller than *digbyana*, with red marks in the throat of the flower, which appears in the autumn. Like *digbyana*, it needs 60°F (16°C). It is found naturally in various areas of Central America.

Brassia

Central America

This tropical epiphytic genus is characterised by a lot of large, spidery shaped flowers, that tend to form on long spikes. Colours vary from yellow to pale green, barred with brown. These orchids have quite large pseudobulbs, with two to four leaves up to 15″ in length. Brassias do best grown in baskets or on bark, and will tolerate temperatures down to 50–60°F (10–16°C). The level of temperature should be kept up during the period of growth, but the plant should be rested after flowering in the autumn (fall). It prefers shady conditions, fairly moist.

SPECIES

B. caudata has 4″ pseudobulbs and 10″ leaves. The flower spike is some 2′ long, and bears up to fourteen large, spidery flowers arranged in two rows. The sepals are up to 4″ long, yellowish green in colour, with dark-brown markings. The yellow lip is pointed with greenish-brown spots. This is a very attractive orchid, which flowers in summer. The minimum temperature should be 55°F (13°C).

B. longissima has huge flowers with sepals up to 10″ long. They are orange-yellow with brown spots. The lip is yellow spotted with red. Temperatures must be maintained at least at 60°F (16°C). This one comes from Mexico.

B. maculata is similar to *B. caudata* with twelve to fourteen yellowish-green flowers spotted brown. The sepals are up to 4″ long, with shorter petals. The lip of the species is whitish in colour, dotted with purple. *B. maculata* will grow in temperatures down to 55°F (13°C), and comes from Jamaica.

Cattleya
South America

The Cattleya genus was named after the pioneer orchid-grower William Cattley. It was first introduced into England in 1815, in America probably when orchid-growing became established around the beginning of the 20th century. This group of orchids is one of the most popular with

Brassavola nodosa has cylindrical leaves, and 3″ flowers with long, thin petals and a white lip. Normally grown on a piece of bark, this show example is being grown in a pot, but the aerial roots can be seen clinging to the outside. B. cucullata is similar in appearance.

growers all over the world, not least because of the ease with which it hybridises. It is spectacular in appearance, and when people think of 'chocolate box' orchids, it is as likely as not Cattleyas that they have in mind. The flowering time depends on the species.

They are epiphytic, with long pseudobulbs covered with a membraneous sheath. The sheath, which is there for the protection of the growing bulb and leaves, is green to begin with, but with time it turns white and on reaching maturity takes on a papery quality. The long, thin pseudobulbs are topped with one, or sometimes a pair of thick, leathery leaves up to 2″ in width. The orchids with one leaf are known as unifoliates; those with two are known as bifoliates.

It is from the base of the leaf or leaves that the beautiful flowers of the Cattleyas emerge. First of all a thin sheath appears. This gradually swells as the embryo buds grow inside. Then the sheath splits open to allow the flower buds, anything from one to twelve in number, to escape, and the flowers to open. Sometimes the flowers are $\frac{1}{2}$″ in diameter—for example with the *luteola*; sometimes, as in some of the modern hybrids, they are up to 8″ across. The flowers have two large petals, with three smaller sepals. The third petal, the lip, is usually very large and brightly coloured.

In natural conditions the Cattleyas grow mainly on branches and rocks towards the edges of forests. Grown under glass, they can be among the most rewarding plants for the amateur. They need moist, light, airy conditions, with a minimum temperature for most species of 60°F (16°C). They are suitable for cultivation in greenhouse or plantarium, or even in the home, given fairly high humidity. However, direct sunlight must not be allowed to scorch the foliage.

With careful selection of plants one can build a collection in which at least some are in flower throughout the year—so these can be very rewarding orchids for the enthusiast; many amateurs specialise in them, as I do myself. The unifoliates have the more showy flowers, while the bifoliates have smaller flowers, although more of them. The colours cover a wide range, including pure white, mauve, pink and yellow, with either similar or contrasting lips. Many species have brighter-coloured spots, and at least one shows a marvellous display of lavender-coloured petals splashed with purple.

Cattleyas grow particularly well in bark mixes, and a fine specimen in a large pot or box, bearing thirty to forty flowers, is a magnificent sight. Of course, most amateurs have only limited space in which to grow their plants, and many people are inclined to prefer as wide a selection as possible of different plants, rather than a smaller range of larger ones. Cattleyas certainly can come into the category of larger orchids—some are recorded as having been grown in England in 1895 bearing 120–200 pseudobulbs. A hybrid, *C.* Portia (*C. bowringiana* × *C. labiata*), was exhibited in 1948 at the Royal Horticultural Society: this had over 250 flowers. In 1954 the same plant measured nearly six feet across, and carried 770 flowers. The plant was originally bought in 1920, and is still growing today, evidence of the robustness characteristic of most orchids given the right conditions.

Many of the Cattleyas described below have been freely used with other genera—Brassavola, Broughtonia, Epidendrum, Laelia, Sophronitis —to create today's hybrids.

SPECIES

C. aclandiae is quite a short member of the Cattleya genus: it is a bifoliate; that is to say, two leaves grow out of the pseudobulb. It has one or two beautiful, brownish-green flowers blotched with purple; the lip is white and pink, with reddish markings in summer. It flowers in autumn (fall) for from four to five weeks. It comes from Brazil.

C. bicolor is a tall bifoliate, 18–24″ in height, with thin pseudobulbs. It flowers in the late summer and autumn (fall) for three to four weeks. The blooms have from four to eight bronze-green petals and a violet-purple lip edged with white. The flower stem is about 8″ long. This one, too, comes from Brazil.

C. bowringiana is between 18–30″ tall, a bifoliate with slender pseudo-bulbs that are usually very swollen at the base. As a result it looks, mis-leadingly, as if there is no rhizome present. The foliage is a distinctive, light, grey-green, and the flowers, of which there may be from eight to twenty in number, are on tall spikes: they are 2½–3″ in diameter, and rose-purple in colour. The lip is deep purple with a creamy throat. This is a variable species—one variety, *C. bowringiana coerula*, is a distinct blue in colour. Many varieties have been used in hybridising to produce flowers of particularly good shape. The species flowers generally for about a month from October to December. As in natural conditions it normally grows near water, it needs plenty of water when cultivated.

C. citrina has recently been re-classified by the International Orchid Nomenclature Committee as *Encyclia citrina*; but as many growers still know it as part of the Cattleya genus, we have included it here for con-venience. This is an unusual plant, in that it grows hanging downwards. The foliage and pseudobulb are of a distinctive blue-green. It is a bi-foliate, with fleshy leaves and beautiful bright-yellow waxy flowers, rather like hanging tulips, 2″ in width and 3″ long, appearing in summer. It is sweetly-scented when in bloom. Originating as it does high in the mountainous region of Mexico, this species appreciates relatively cool conditions, and does extremely well in the draught of a fan, growing on a piece of bark or tree fern.

Cattleya *Gloriette, a typical Cattleya hybrid, with its beautiful colours and distinctive lip. Many collectors specialize in Cattleyas exclusively because different species and hybrids can be flowered all the year round.*

C. dowiana is a unifoliate Cattleya with stout pseudobulbs 15″ high and flowers 6″ in diameter. The petals are gorgeous golden-yellow and the lip, which is very wide and frilled, is crimson-red streaked with gold. In the autumn (fall) there are up to eight of these huge, fragrant flowers, appearing for about five weeks in September or October. The temperature should be kept above 64°F (18°C) for this species, which comes originally from Costa Rica. The variety *C. dowiana var. aurea*, which comes from Colombia, is similar, except that the flowers are pure yellow. Both the species and the variety need plenty of light, and prefer to hang in baskets from the roof. Bear in mind that hanging plants dry out quicker than plants growing on a bench, and therefore an eye must be kept on the need for water. *C. dowiana* has been used extensively in the production of yellow hybrids.

C. forbesii is a delightful plant, bifoliate, with thick pseudobulbs 8–12″ in length. The flowers are 3″ in diameter, three to eight in number, with greeny-yellow petals and a shell-pink lip, beautifully streaked inside with red, which curls over the column. They appear in August, for about six weeks. This is a fast-growing orchid, and soon develops four or five heads. The colour is somewhat variable—the greener varieties are specially coveted. Brazil is its place of origin.

C. granulosa is another fine bifoliate with 12–20″ pseudobulbs which are distinctly noded. The colour of the flowers, which appear in the autumn (fall), varies from olive-green to yellow, with brown spots either few or many in number. The lip is flat and spreading, and may be rose-pink or white, depending on the variety. This one too comes from Brazil.

C. guttata var. leopoldii is a tall, thin bifoliate, 20–24″ in height. It has from four to twelve waxy, crimson flowers spotted with bronze, 3″ in diameter and with a small, spade-shaped, crimson-purple lip. This is a very free-flowering species and revels in plenty of light; it flowers in the summer, and originates from Brazil. (The variety *alba* has green petals and a white lip, and is another very attractive plant suitable for the beginner.)

C. intermedia is a very variable species. It is a bifoliate with slender pseudobulbs and three to six clusters of flowers 4″ in diameter. These are generally rose-coloured with a purple lip. There are many named variations on this theme—the following varieties are just four of them: *alba* has pure white flowers; *amethystina* pink flowers with an amethyst lip; *aquinii* rose flowers with purple splashes on both petals and lip; *lilaczina* all-lilac flowers. The species flowers in the summer. It grows naturally in Brazil.

C. labiata is a beautiful unifoliate Cattleya with 6″ clusters of mauve-pink flowers with a large crimson-magenta lip. They appear generally in the winter. The exact colour is very variable, and many plants which have

Cattleya forbesii *from Brazil.*

carried different names in the past have been proved to be varieties of
C. labiata. Examples are *C. gaskelliana, C. lawrenceana, C. mossiae,
C. schroederae,* and *C. warneri.* Many of these have white or bi-coloured
forms, and these are now known as *C. labiata var.*—. No doubt the use of
these names in the past will cause confusion in times to come, when past
records are used in establishing hybrids.

C. loddigesii is a summer- or autumn (fall)-flowering bifoliate with pseudobulbs 15–20″ in length. When it blooms there are two to four waxy
flowers 4″ in diameter, pale mauve with a paler lip. The flowers are very
substantial. The white variety, *alba,* is extremely rare. The country of
origin is Brazil.

C. luteola is a charming, dwarf Brazilian Cattleya with short 8″ pseudobulbs and clusters of 1½″ lemon-yellow flowers with a whiteish lip
streaked with purple. This is an attractive, small plant, splendidly suited
for a plantarium.

C. rex is a beautiful species from Peru. The wavy petals are normally
creamy-yellow in colour, the lip is crimson-red, and the throat of the
flower is yellow. Some varieties have rich, buttercup-yellow petals. This
is a unifoliate orchid, with two or three flowers 5″ wide borne on 12–15″
pseudobulbs.

C. schilleriana is an ideal choice for your plantarium: it is a dwarf bifoliate Cattleya with 4–5″ pseudobulbs and clusters of two to four
reddish-brown flowers spotted with dark brown. The flowers appear in
the spring for about six weeks. The flattened, spade-shaped lip is white
with rose shading and stripes. It flowers in the spring. Its place of origin is
Brazil.

C. skinneri is another tall-stemmed bifoliate with small flowers 2–4″ in
diameter, deep-rose in colour with a darker lip, in clusters of up to eight.
There is a very rare white variety, *alba,* which shows yellow in the lip.
Although the flower sheaths are formed in the autumn, flowers rarely
appear until April or May, so do not cut off the sheath thinking it is not
going to flower. *C. skinneri* comes originally from Mexico and Guatemala.

C. trianaei bears two or three large flowers. These are 6″ in diameter,
mauve in colour with a frilled, crimson-purple lip. It is a unifoliate, and
the pseudobulbs are about 15″ long. The flowers appear in December and
January, remaining for about a month—and so this is a useful, Christmas-
flowering orchid. The precise colour of the flowers is very variable;
many named varieties were formerly available, but they are becoming
scarce now. This species comes from Colombia.

C. velutina is a dwarf bifoliate plant with thin, pseudobulbs 8–10″ in length. The flowers are 4″ in diameter, orange-brown in colour with deep-red spots. The lip is flat and spade-shaped, white with mauve veining and a yellow tip. The whole plant has a very waxy-looking appearance, and flowers in August for about a month. It comes from Brazil.

C. walkeriana is another dwarf, unifoliate Cattleya with short (3″-long), stubby pseudobulbs, carrying one or two rose-purple, sweetly-scented flowers with a deep-rose coloured, spade-shaped lip. The variety *alba* is pure white in colour, while the variety *nobilior* is lavender with a darker lip. It flowers for about six weeks in the autumn (fall). Its country of origin is Brazil.

Coelogyne
Far East

As its Latin name implies to the initiated, these are hollow, bulbous orchids growing on short rhizomes, so short that they are sometimes indiscernible. There are one or two leaves on each pseudobulb; these

Coelogyne ochracea, one of the sweetest-scented species, and highly recommended for beginners. This is a typical example.

Ophrys apifera, *the 'bee orchid', growing in the wild. Orchid-lovers must always be aware of the need to conserve wild-growing species both at home and abroad.*

are evergreen and last for three or four years. The size of the plants varies; some species have 2″ pseudobulbs, others as much as 6″. Leaves show a similar variety, but are usually thick and fleshy. The flowers are usually white, sometimes bronze, and free-flowering. The flower-spikes are produced before the pseudobulbs are fully grown.

This is a somewhat cooler-growing genus than some, originating at quite high altitudes in India and the Far East. Most Coelogynes flower in the spring for three or four weeks. They should be rested in winter.

SPECIES

C. cristata is a cool-growing plant that quickly makes a remarkable specimen. The fat pseudobulbs are some 2″ long; the white flowers, 3″ in diameter, grow from the base of the pseudobulbs, as many as six to a stem. A large plant can therefore carry sixty or more flowers. The variety *lemoniana* has a yellow blotch in the lip. This species needs a temperature of only 50°F (10°C) or more; and so it can often be hung outside during the summer, in the shade of a tree. It does best in pans or baskets and resents disturbance. Fresh compost should be pushed between the pseudobulbs

when needed. The flower buds are covered with a brownish bract which should not be disturbed—it is here that flowers will appear. The plant should be rested to the point of shrivelling in summer, but should be watered well when growth recommences. *C. cristata* comes originally from India.

C. ochracea is a dwarf species (8″ high) with short pseudobulbs topped by two hard, dark-green leaves. Flower stems are freely produced—they are about 10″ high and carry from six to ten white flowers $\frac{1}{2}$″ in diameter with a yellow-orange blotched lip. A plant in a 3″ pot can produce twenty flowers or more in the spring. *C. ochracea* needs a temperature of at least 50°F (10°C), and should be rested during the winter. It comes originally from India.

C. pandurata is a beautiful lime-green-flowered species needing a temperature of 60°F (16°C) or more. Its large pseudobulbs, 24″ long, grow on thick rhizomes. The leaves are broad and long, some 18″. The 24″ flower spike carries up to fourteen flowers in pairs. The flowers are about 3″ in diameter, bright green in colour, flecked and streaked with black markings. This lovely orchid, which comes from Borneo, does best in a long basket or pan, as the rhizome grows forward towards the light.

Cymbidium

Far East

Boat-shaped rivals to the Cattleyas in the popularity stakes, Cymbidiums must be the most hybridised orchids today. Thousands of crosses have been made and today's flowers are far removed from the original species, which are not often seen now. They are semi-terrestrial and easy to cultivate, produce anything up to thirty flowers per stem and only require a temperature of 50°F (10°C). Many collections are composed entirely of Cymbidium hybrids. Cymbidiums are in general spring-flowering, with very long-lasting flowers, persisting for up to twelve weeks.

Coming from high altitudes in the Himalayas and Burma, Cymbidiums are ideally suitable for growing in most places throughout the world in a compost similar to that for Paphiopedilums, that is a mixture of bark, sphagnum moss and charcoal. Cymbidiums soon become large plants, given regular feeding while in growth until the flower spikes appear from the base of the pseudobulbs in the late autumn (fall); watering should then be reduced and feeding stopped. A natural fertiliser based on seaweed is the preferred kind—some of the chemical fertilisers can burn the thick, fleshy roots. Cymbidiums need ample light and plants grown in large houses with fans to create heavy air movement will need less shading during sunny weather. The plants can be grown in beds out-doors in many parts of the USA, but care must be taken to see that frost does not touch them. A minimum temperature of 48°F (9°C) is sufficient. Plants benefit from overhead spraying during hot weather.

SPECIES

C. devonianum is a delightful, small-growing plant with leaves ½" wide and 12" high. The flower spikes are pendulous (hang down over the edge of the container) and will each carry twenty 1" flowers coloured olive-green with crimson lines and a purple-crimson lip. Numerous flower spikes appear on a well-grown plant. Care must be taken not to break them when you move the plant. India is its place of origin.

C. giganteum is a very strong-growing plant. The leaves are gigantic, 2–3′ long, the flower spike is about 2′ in length carrying ten to twenty yellowy-green flowers 4" in diameter. The greenish-yellow lip is marked with bright crimson. This is a very fragrant orchid, which comes from India.

C. insigne has long, 2′ 6" leaves, 1" wide, and a very long flower spike 3′ in length. This carries twenty pinkish-white flowers 3½–4" in diameter; the lips are red with purple spots. This species is a parent of most of today's hybrids. It comes from India.

C. lowianum has beautiful green-yellow 4" diameter flowers on several graceful, arching spikes up to 2′ long. There may be from ten to twenty-five long-lasting flowers on each spike. The lip of the flower is creamy with scarlet spots. *C. lowianum* comes from Burma.

Dendrobium

Far East and Australasia

This genus is a tree-dweller, one of the largest of the orchid family and one of the most variable in growth and flowers. All the species are epi-phytic and flower very freely, many are deciduous or semi-deciduous while others retain their leaves. Most flower in the spring, for some six or eight weeks.

The deciduous plants usually produce three or four new pseudobulbs, or cane-type stems each year, anything from 1′ to 4′ high with pairs of leaves opposite one another when growth is completed. Ultimately a terminal leaf is produced; watering should then be reduced until the

flower buds are seen to be developing. If water and heat is given too soon after that, new growths will develop instead of flower buds. A temperature of 60°F (16°C) is ideal while plants are growing but should be reduced to 50°F (10°C) in the autumn (fall) and winter until buds are seen, when it is taken back up to the higher figure.

The evergreen Dendrobiums have thicker, club-shaped rather than cane-like pseudobulbs and do not flower all down them. They usually put out upright, arching flower-spikes, with leaves, mainly at the tops of the pseudobulbs. They are all spectacular when in flower.

Best grown in a moisture-retentive compost, Dendrobiums thrive in good light and plenty of moisture. Beware of strong sunlight directly on the new growth for this will quickly burn and fold over.

Flowers, which vary tremendously in shape, range in colour from white, purple, and plum to yellow and a mixture of all these colours. A well-grown plant should flower the whole length of the stem. Do not cut off old leafless canes as these will also produce flowers.

SPECIES

D. aggregatum is a delightful dwarf-growing, evergreen plant with short, 2″ pseudobulbs and a single leaf on top. Up to twenty flat, golden-yellow flowers, 1″ across, appear on an arching spike in the late spring or early summer. They are sweetly-scented. The species is best grown on a piece of bark or raft. It comes from India.

D. arachnites is a dwarf plant up to 12″ high with slender pseudobulbs. The bright orange flowers 1½″ long give one the impression of a cluster of small birds. It comes from Burma, and Malaysia, and flowers in the spring for about a month.

D. chrysotoxum is an evergreen with 10″ club-shaped pseudobulbs and with leaves 5″ in length. The flowers come from the top of the bulbs in drooping masses of golden-yellow with deep-orange throats and fringed lips giving the appearance of bunches of grapes. Plants need rest when new bulbs are fully grown. This species flowers in late spring, and comes from India.

D. densiflorum, from India, is an evergreen up to 20″ tall with thick pseudobulbs. It is a very similar plant to *D. chrysotoxum*, except that it has denser, brighter, clear-yellow flowers with deeper-orange throats. The plant should be rested during the winter.

D. infundibulum is an evergreen with dark, black, hairy, pseudobulbs up to 24″ long. The pure-white, trumpet-shaped flowers are 2–3″ across with a yellow stain on the lip. The species normally flowers in the spring but can be unpredictable. It comes from India.

Dendrobium infundibulum, *with its beautiful, white flowers, which show a yellow mark on the lip.*

D. kingianum is an evergreen with 15″ sharply-pointed pseudobulbs and 3–6″ leaves. The terminal spikes carry a multitude of $\frac{1}{2}$″ violet-to-pink coloured flowers. Coming from Australia, it likes plenty of light and dry conditions. The variety *alba* has pure-white flowers.

D. nobile is a deciduous, variable, cane type, growing from 18″ to 4′ tall. It flowers from the nodes where leaves have fallen from the canes. It likes plenty of water and heat during summer but cooler and dryer conditions when growth stops in winter. The flowers appear in spring. They are up to 3″ in size, mauve-and-white with a deeper mauve blotch in the lip. Individual plants differ considerably in colour. There are many fine, named varieties. It comes from India.

D. nobile var. virginalis is similar to *D. nobile*, except that it is only 20″ high and the flowers are a glistening, pure white.

D. phalaenopsis is an evergreen with long pseudobulbs—up to 3′ long. This warmer-growing species has a terminal spike 12–20″ long with from ten to fifteen 3″ flowers that range from white to deep-purple, with a darker lip. It is very suitable for cutting. *D. phalaenopsis* comes from Australia. It requires a temperature some 5°F warmer than most of the other Dendrobium species.

Laelia

South America

This genus is very similar in appearance to Cattleya, except that the flowers are somewhat smaller and narrower. There are, however, more of them on each spike. The pseudobulbs can be short and fat or long and thin. The flowers are produced on long stems, generally from the top of the pseudobulbs, and can be purple, red, yellow, white or purple-and-white, varying in size from 1″ to 6″.

Laelias appreciate slightly cooler conditions than Cattleyas and a little more light. As they are epiphytic, a place hanging near the glass at the coolest end of the Cattleya house suits them very well. They will grow in temperatures down to 55–60°F (13–16°C), depending on the species.

Laelias have been crossed with many other genera such as Cattleya, Brassavola, Broughtonia, and Sophronitis; and also with more than one at the same time, to give multi-generic crosses. The resulting hybrids have all gained from their Laelia parentage.

SPECIES

L. anceps is a popular species which will quickly make a specimen plant. Colours are very variable, ranging from a pure white to various shades of lavender. The flowers, from six to eight in number, are 4″ across with a yellow-throated lip; they grow on thin spikes, up to 24″ long, from the top of the pseudobulb. From the short, fat, angular pseudobulbs grow single thick, fleshy, leaves, some 12″ long. The rhizome tends to grow towards the light in a forward and upward direction, creating a need for frequent repotting. This can be avoided by periodically turning the plant by 45°, so as to contain the rhizome in the pot. The species needs a temperature of at least 55° and flowers in the period November to January. There are numerous named varieties worth looking for. *L. anceps* comes from Mexico.

L. autumnalis is similar to *L. anceps*, but has eight to ten paler flowers and two or three leaves to each pseudobulb. It too needs a temperature of at least 55°F (13°C), and is a winter-flowering species. It comes from Mexico.

L. cinnabarina has its natural home in Brazil, and needs a temperature of at least 60°F (16°C). It has 8–10″ pseudobulbs that are swollen at the base and taper towards the top, and carry one or two 6″ leaves, from which appear 12″ erect spikes carrying from eight to fifteen orange-red flowers $1\frac{1}{2}$″ across. The flowering time is from March to May. The variety *cowanii*, as it is well-known to many growers, has pure yellow flowers, and has now been officially renamed *L. flava*.

L. gouldiana is very similar to *L. anceps* except that the pseudobulbs are a little larger, the flowers are rounder in shape and bright purple in colour, and the lip is slightly darker. It is held by some to be a naturally occurring hybrid of *L. anceps* and *L. autumnalis*.

L. grandis has thin pseudobulbs, 8–10″ long, with a single 6″ leaf. Each flower spike carries from three to six yellow-brown flowers 4″ in diameter with a white lip, with rose-coloured markings. The flowering time is May to June. It comes from Brazil, and needs a temperature of 60°F (16°C).

L. milleri is a fairly 'new' orchid—it was first found in 1957. It is a small-growing plant with 2″ pseudobulbs; from each grows a single leaf 3″ long, and an erect spike carrying from six to eight brilliant red flowers. This species was found growing on ironstone rock—it does best in full sun. This is a warmer-growing Laelia—60°F (16°C).

L. pumila is a beautiful, dwarf Brazilian species. It has small, thin pseudobulbs 1½" long with a single 1½" leaf. The one or two flowers produced on a short spike are up to 3" across with broad, overlapping petals of rose-purple, and a darker red-purple lip marked yellow in the throat. The flowers appear in the autumn (fall). This is a gem of an orchid and very suitable for a plantarium. It is sometimes listed in catalogues as *L. praestans*. A temperature of at least 55°F (13°C) must be maintained.

L. purpurata is a tall-growing plant from Brazil, with bi-coloured flowers. The slender pseudobulbs are 24–30" long, and the flowers, pale-rose in colour, have a crimson-purple lip with a yellow throat. It flowers in the period May to August. It is one of the cooler-growing Laelias.

L. xanthina is another tall-growing plant, with slender pseudobulbs 20" long and yellow flowers 3" in diameter. The lip is edged white and veined with crimson-purple. This species flowers in June, with three or four flowers per spike, and needs at least 60°F (16°C).

Lycaste

Central and South America

This easily-grown genus, supposedly named after a young Sicilian beauty, is mainly epiphytic. It has shiny green, ovoid pseudobulbs, 1–3" high and topped by one to four fairly large, plicated leaves on short stems. The leaves are anything from 1" to 4" wide, extending to 18" high and very fleshy. They abhor water on them.

The flowers are glorious, and are produced singularly from the base of the pseudobulbs on short stems with small leaf-like bracts, and can be white, yellow, pink or green. They are very showy and last for up to five weeks; eight to ten single stems can show on a small plant in winter and spring. Coming originally from fairly high, cool altitudes, Lycastes need a temperature of 60°F (16°C) in a shady, moist position. New growths develop in the spring, when frequent watering with weak fertiliser should be given; come late autumn (fall) and many of the leaves will turn brown and drop, when less water should be given. The flower spikes develop at about this time and care should be taken, in order to avoid damping off, not to wet the buds.

Plants can be grown into large specimens, and do well indoors. This genus has been used to create the beautiful Angulocastes, 'Apollo' and 'Auburn'.

L. aromatica, from Mexico, has pseudobulbs 4″ high and 8–10″ leaves. Many fragrant yellow flowers, $2\frac{1}{2}$″ in diameter, with an orange-spotted lip, grow on 6″ stems in March, April and May.

L. deppei, from Guatemala, has large, 4″ flowers with pale-green sepals spotted with red, white petals, and a bright-yellow lip marked with red. The length of the flower stems is about 8″; that of the leaves, some 12–15″; the foliage is greyish-green. The flowers appear in winter.

L. locusta is an unusual-coloured orchid—it is green; so much so that the flowers are almost indistinguishable from the leaves. Flowering in April– May, the $3\frac{1}{2}$″ flowers are apple-green with the exception of the white column. The leaves are 18″ long, and the flower stem some 12″. *L. locusta* comes from Peru.

L. tricolor, from Costa Rica, is another free-flowering species; the leaves grow to 18″, with 4″ creamy-white flowers coloured with shades of apple-green and rose. This is a highly-desirable but scarce plant, which flowers in May–June.

L. virginalis is the truly beautiful national flower of Guatemala. It is very variable; the flowers range in colour from white to dark pink; the lip is darker. They are rather waxy, and about 6″ in diameter. Winter is the flowering time of this species, which has leaves some 15–18″ in length.

Odontoglossum

Central America

This is a large family of orchids, usually divided into two groups, Mexican and Colombian. The latter require cooler conditions with high humidity, coming as they do from the cloud forest regions; the ones described below fall into this group. They require a minimum temperature of 55°F (13°C), with a maximum of 75°F (27°C), during summer. Plenty of humidity, moving fresh air and shade suits these lovely orchids.

O. cervantesii is a dwarf plant. The pseudobulbs are seen in clusters 1″ high, and the single leaves are 2″ long. The flowers grow on 6″ pendulous spikes; there are usually from two to six of them in the spring, round and white with concentric ring-like markings in spring of a dull, crimson brown. Some varieties have pale, rose-coloured flowers instead of white. This is an easily grown orchid which should be rested during winter. It comes from Mexico.

OPPOSITE
The beautiful Odontoglossum grande, *with its yellow flowers marked with brown.*

O. crispum is an extremely variable species with flowers ranging in colour from pure crisp white to pale rose; they have a yellow crest on the lip. The flowers are large, star-shaped, and up to $3\frac{1}{2}''$ in diameter—there are up to twenty on each flower spike. Many varieties of this species have been crossed and many fine new pure-white, spotted and yellow varieties have been bred. One example, bred by the English firm of Charlesworth, has been named 'Crispum Premier'. This has beautiful, round, white flowers, some with a few purplish spots.

O. grande, from Guatemala, but considered one of the 'Mexican' group, is one of the most popular and attractive orchids you can grow. It has large pseudobulbs 4″ long with two grey-green leathery leaves. From the base of the leaves grow flower spikes 10–12″ long. On each flower spike are from two to six waxy-yellow flowers 4–6″ in diameter, banded and blotched with chestnut brown. The small lip is creamy white or yellow, spotted with brown in the autumn. It is because of its markings that this is sometimes called the 'clown orchid'. This plant should be given complete rest after flowering, until new growth appears at the base of the pseudo-bulbs.

O. pulchellum is a small-growing species with oval pseudobulbs $1\frac{1}{2}''$ high and grass-like leaves. It is commonly called the Lily-of-the-valley orchid. It has erect spikes with small, round, waxy flowers, pure crystalline white with a yellow crest on the lip. This very fragrant species flowers during the winter. It comes from Guatemala.

Oncidium

South America

This is one of the loveliest orchid genera. The flowers, very variable in size and shape, are mainly bright yellow marked with brown. The tall stems are often branched, carrying from one to over a hundred flowers, which can be likened to myriads of small butterflies, and this is why Oncidiums are referred to as 'butterfly orchids'. They are epiphytic, and do well on pieces of bark or tree fern. They need a fair amount of sunshine (although not so much that the foliage is scorched), high humidity, and plenty of fresh air. The minimum temperature required is from $52°$F $(11°$C$)$ to $60°$F $(16°$C$)$, depending on the species.

Oncidiums are so prolific in their flowering that it is advisable to cut the spikes after three weeks, and place them into water so as to give the plant a chance to build up for another year. Oncidiums can be grown outdoors in many parts of the USA and do well in beds under lath-houses.

O. cheirophorum, which flowers in the summer for three or four weeks, is a delightful dwarf plant, ideal for small plantaria. The shiny pseudobulbs are only $\frac{1}{2}''$ long, and the leaves 2″. The thin flower spike is up to 4″ long, and branched to carry numerous small showy, bright-yellow flowers only $\frac{1}{4}''$ diameter. These are very fragrant in autumn. The minimum temperature for this species is 52°F (11°C), so this is at the cooler end of the range. It needs plenty of moisture when growing, but in winter only enough to prevent bulbs from shrivelling. It comes from Costa Rica.

O. concolor has pseudobulbs 1″ long with two or three leaves. The flower spike is 6–8″ long, while the flowers themselves are yellow in colour, 2″ in diameter, with a large, lemon-yellow lip. This species, one of the cooler-growing, is truly spectacular in flower.

O. flexuosum has two leaves 6″ long growing from each 2″ pseudobulb. The flower spike is tall, thin and wiry, and in summer carries many bright-yellow flowers, $\frac{1}{2}''$ in diameter. This species is suitable for bark or tree-fern culture, and needs a temperature of at least 55°F (13°C). It comes from Brazil, and flowers in the spring and summer.

O. forbesii has small pseudobulbs, from each of which grows a single leaf 8″ long. The large flower spike is 18″ long, with many chestnut-brown, waxy flowers 2″ in diameter with narrow, bright-yellow margins. This is a very handsome species, which requires a minimum temperature of 55–60°F (13–16°C), according to species. It flowers in the late summer and autumn. Brazil is its country of origin.

O. kramerianum is a spectacular-flowering orchid from Ecuador. It has flat, wrinkled pseudobulbs from which grows a single, dark green leaf. The pseudobulbs are very hard and leathery. The slender, tall flower stem, which can be 2–4′ long, produces one flower after another, each lasting from two to three weeks. The sepals and petals are narrow and about 3″ long; they are yellow, heavily marked with reddish brown. The lip is canary yellow with brown spots, and looks like some weird butterfly. Flowers are produced continuously over a period of a year. *O. kramerianum* needs a minimum temperature of 60°F (16°C). The species *O. papilio* is very similar to it.

O. longipes is another dwarf-growing plant with 1″ pseudobulbs and 4″ spikes each carrying from one to five 1″ flowers, brown and yellow in colour, with a white lip. It needs a temperature of 60°F (16°C) and flowers in the late summer.

O. ornithorrhynchum has oval pseudobulbs with 8″ leaves. It is a bifoliate— that is, two leaves grow from each pseudobulb. The flowers are small— $\frac{1}{4}''$ in diameter, rosy lilac-pink, with tiny yellow centres. They grow on

Oncidium flexuosum, *a spring- and summer-flowering species from Brazil.*

arching spikes 18–24″ long. This is a very free-flowering orchid, and a well-grown plant can produce hundreds of flowers in late autumn. It requires a minimum temperature of 55°F (13°C), and high humidity in the growing period. Guatemala is its country of origin.

Paphiopedilum

Far East

Here we have the aristocrats of the orchid world, distinguished by their characteristic lip, which is pouch-shaped. From this comes the Paphiopedilum's common name, 'slipper orchid'. They are also known to many growers under the generic name 'Cypripedium', but true Cypripediums come from colder countries, and they die down in the winter. They are useful for growing in rockeries in the garden. The Paphiopedilums come from tropical countries, they are not deciduous and can be split into two types, those with plain green foliage, and those with spotted leaves. Both types are semi-terrestrial—they will live either in the ground or on rocks. When living on rocks the roots adapt to the need for gaining nutrition from the air, becoming in time noticeably less hairy. The plain-leaved type will tolerate a minimum temperature of 60°F (16°C), whereas the spotted- or mottled-leaved type requires a higher temperature, at least 65°F (18°C). Paphiopedilums are relatively easy to grow, especially suitable for indoor locations and plantariums.

Both types are bulbless, having a short, fleshy, underground stem, from which grow the distichous (arranged in two rows) leaves, usually six or more in number. From the centre of the leaves the flower stem emerges, normally carrying a single flower, variable in colour. A few varieties carry more. The flowers have a large, flat, spotted sepal known as the dorsal sepal, and narrow, spotted petals; the lip is characteristically slipper-shaped with a waxy, polished appearance. Many species have hairy and wart-like appendages on the petals. Paphiopedilums are very variable as to size and shape—they are recognised by their pouch-shaped lip.

Being semi-terrestrial, Paphiopedilums need a more moisture-retentive compost than purely epiphytic orchids. A good mixture is bark, sphagnum moss and charcoal. Many species come from limestone districts, so the addition of a few pieces of limestone is essential to these. In the absence of pseudobulbs Paphiopedilums need a fair amount of water when growing and must never be allowed to dry right out. On the other hand they must not be kept sodden wet. A fair amount of shade is necessary—no direct sunlight in summer.

Atmospheric moisture is important, but avoid a close, stuffy atmosphere. Plants can develop multiple growths sufficient to fill a 10″ pot, carrying twenty or more flowers. Although species are not often seen today, a tremendous amount of hybridising has been done with Paphiopedilums, the aim being to produce very large, round, colourful flowers. Fortunately for the grower with limited space, there has also been a considerable interest recently in the species with the smaller flower, and many nurserymen have this aim in mind. All Paphiopedilums are very long-lasting, remaining in flower for four to eight weeks, generally in the period November–March.

SPECIES

P. acmodontum is a mottled-leaf type, with 15″ flower spikes carrying one flower with a green-and-rose dorsal and sepals, with a greenish-brown pouch. The flower is about 4″ in diameter, and appears from January to March. Malaysia is its place of origin.

P. argus, which comes from the Philippines, is a very showy mottled-foliage Paphiopedilum. The flower spikes are 14–18″ long, the hairy stems carrying greenish flowers 5″ in diameter, with a white dorsal petal striped with purple. The flower colour is in fact quite variable. The pouch is purple-brown in colour, while the petals are pinkish near the tip, and spotted with dark-purple hairy warts. The flowers last for eight to ten weeks during the summer. This species needs a temperature of at least 62°F (17°C).

P. bellatulum has mottled foliage, and delightful 2″ round, creamy-white flowers covered in purple spots. The flowers are carried on short, 3″ stems. An almost pure-white variety exists, and there are others which vary tremendously in their markings. *P. bellatulum* flowers generally in the period January to March. It is a good choice for a plantarium.

P. callosum has mottled foliage; the striking 3½″ flower has a large, white dorsal striped and flushed with purple; it has pale-green petals with black warts, and a polished brown-and-purple pouch. Occasionally two flowers are produced on one stem. It can bloom at any time, sometimes more than once a year, and remains in bloom for two or three months. It comes from Malaysia.

P. concolor, from Burma, has mottled foliage and 2–3″ creamy-white flowers, covered with tiny red dots, on 2″ stems. It flowers in late summer. This is a small plant suitable for inclusion in a plantarium.

OPPOSITE
Paphiopedilum purpuratum *from the Philippines—note the large dorsal sepal, and the deep purplish-red lip.*

P. delenatii has greyish, mottled foliage and 10″ stems which carry one or two delightful, white flowers flushed with pink. The pouch is rose-pink. This species can flower at almost any time of the year, for almost three months. Indo-China is its place of origin.

P. fairieanum is an unusual-looking orchid with all-green foliage and double-curved petals that turn upwards at the ends. The petals, including the dorsal petal, are white veined with purple; the pouch is green, and flushed with red. This species flowers generally in the autumn (fall). It comes from India.

P. glaucophyllum is another green-foliage plant, this time from Malaysia. The blossoms are dark-green with a white-edged lip, the petals brownish-green, twisted in shape with black, hairy edges. The pouch is purple and yellow. When this species produces new flowers, they appear at the end of the existing flower stem.

P. godefroyae, from Siam, is a small, mottled-leaf type with delightful, white flowers 3″ in diameter. These are spotted and marked with dark, mauvish brown. This species, which blooms in the summer, often produces more than one flower per stem.

P. insigne is a cool-growing, plain-leaved plant that most beginners start with. It has a whitish sepal overlaid with purple spots, with greenish-yellow petals striped and spotted brown. The pouch is pale reddish-brown. The flower of the variety *sandarae* is all greeny-yellow with a white edge. *P. insigne* is the most popular species of Paphiopedilum— hundreds are grown for use as cut flowers in the Christmas period. A large well-grown plant will carry twenty or more flowers, and tolerate temperatures lower than most orchids—down to 50°F (10°C).

P. Maudiae is in fact not a species, but a hybrid. It is a lovely plant, one of the most popular grown today. The Maudiae type are warm-growing, requiring a minimum of 65°F (18°C). They have beautiful, mottled foliage up to 8″ long and 2″ wide, the elegant flowers usually white or green. The colour varies somewhat with each named variety, but generally they have a large, white, dorsal sepal with green stripes, a creamy-white pouch varying in colour sometimes towards green, and narrow greenish-white petals with various small wart-like appendages. The flowers are borne on long 8–14″ hairy stems, and last up to ten weeks, usually during the summer but often at other times of the year; well-grown plants often flower twice a year. This is an ideal choice for a plantarium.

P. purpuratum has beautiful 3″ flowers with petals of a deep, purple red, and a purple lip. The 1″ dorsal sepal is white with purple lines. This species, which comes from the Philippines, flowers generally in the August-November period, and soon grows into a fine specimen.

Phragmipedium
Peru

These beautiful terrestrial orchids have the fascinating long petals mentioned in Chapter Two. Very similar in appearance to the Paphiopedilums, they have the same type of pouched lip, and also have no pseudobulbs. However, they are more robust, making multiple tuft-like growths of longish strap-shaped leaves. The long flower spikes carry one or more pinkish-to-creamy-white flowers 2–6″ across, the two lateral petals on some species extending in ribbon-like fashion up to 3′ in length. These lateral petals can grow at the astonishing rate of 1″ a day.

SPECIES

P. caudatum has leaves 10–18″ long, 1″ wide. The flower spike is covered with down; it is up to 30″ long, and carries from one to four flowers. These have a creamy-white dorsal with greenish veining. The sepals are brownish-red; the lateral petals are ribbon-like and twisted—they are up to 3′ long and shaded yellow. The lip is bronze-green. The long petals give the flower a Chinese mandarin appearance, but their shape is to enable a ground insect to climb up and pollinate the flower. Close examination will show that the lower part of the petals is covered in tiny hairs for the insects to grip. This species flowers from March to August, and requires a temperature of 60°F (16°C). It should be kept fairly moist in summer but drier in winter. It should not be allowed to get bone dry, however.

P. longifolium, as the name implies, bears long leaves, 2′ long and 1″ wide. The flower spike, 3′ long, bears from eight to twelve flowers, 6″ in diameter. The dorsal petal is light-green flushed with purplish-rose; the pouch is yellowish-green spotted with rose; the petals are twisted, green and rose in colour. This species, which flowers from March to May, requires a minimum temperature of 60°F (16°C).

Other species exist and have been crossed with the above to give some fine hybrids. Some of the crosses were made some years ago, and are hard to obtain. But the following example is available.

P. Sedenii (P. longifolium × P. schlimii) is a hybrid: it has 10″-long leaves ½″ wide, and a 12″ spike of delightful pink-and-white flowers with a white dorsal striped with green. The pouch is pink spotted with red inside. This is a strong-growing plant needing 60°F (16°C) with ample watering during the growing period. Less water is required in winter. It flowers in the period March to September.

Sobralia

Central America

This is a tallish, reed-like orchid. It is terrestrial and grows naturally in the more open fringe areas of the forests of Central America.

Sobralias require good light and plenty of moisture when growing, with ample fresh air. They delight in the breeze from a fan, but require a minimum temperature of 60°F (16°C). Their size can vary from 18″ to 6′.

Phalaenopsis amabilis, a white 'moth orchid'; from this species many fine hybrids with 5″ flowers have been obtained.

Phalaenopsis schilleriana, *a pink 'moth orchid'. The photograph shows clearly how the petal forming the lip differs from the others.*

The stems are thin and reed-like, and the plants have plaited leaves up to 8″ long that remain for many years. The plants can be mistaken for bamboo when not in flower. Large flowers, rather like Cattleyas, and up to 6″ across, are produced from the tips of the canes in the summer, but only last a day or so and are not suitable for cutting; but immediately one dies another bud takes its place, as many as eight flowers from each cane being produced.

Sobralias do need rather large containers; 8–10″ pots or tubs will soon fill up with these vigorous plants. New growths develop from the base after the plant has flowered and grow quite quickly. Older canes that have lost their leaves should be cut off at ground-level.

SPECIES

S. decora has stems up to 2′ high with 3″ flowers. The petals and sepals are creamy-white, and the lip rose-pink.

S. macrantha grows stems up to 6′ high with leaves closer together than the other species. The flowers, rich purple-crimson in colour, and sometimes as much as 6″ in diameter, have a yellowish throat and a frilled edge. There is an all-white variety, *alba*.

S. xantholeuca is very similar in appearance to *macrantha*, except that the flower has wider petals and is sulphur-yellow in colour, with a deeper-yellow lip.

Sophronitis

Brazil

These are dwarf-growing epiphytic orchids suitable for a cooler orchid-house or plantarium. The pseudobulbs are small and thin, with a single fleshy leaf up to 3″ in length. The flowers are generally orange or red, large and flat in shape. They last for up to four weeks.

Sophronitis is best grown on a piece of bark in fairly moist conditions, with plenty of light. A minimum temperature of 55°F (13°C) is required.

SPECIES

S. cernua has flowers about ½″ in diameter in clusters of three or four, and a bright orange in colour. It is summer-flowering.

S. grandiflora is a bigger flowered species, with wider petals a vivid scarlet in colour, as distinct from the bright orange of *S. cernua*. The flowers appear in the autumn (fall).

S. rosea is similar in habit to *S. grandiflora*, but the flowers are a rosy red, appearing in the winter.

Vanda

Far East

These orchids, found in various parts of the world and at various altitudes, are variable in their requirements. They need high humidity and

OPPOSITE
Vanda coerulea, *a monopodial species with fine blue flowers.*

OPPOSITE
Vanda burgeffii, *a hybrid, with typical mottled petal colour.*

moisture levels, as they are epiphytic and produce large amounts of aerial roots; some are quite small-growing, others will grow to 8′ or more. All Vandas are monopodial. They have either V-shaped strap-like leaves, or terete, round leaves; the leaves grow alternately on each side of the stem. Flowers also vary in size from $\frac{1}{2}$″ to 4″ across, and can be yellow, rose, white, brown and blue. They may be spotted, barred, or with a tessellated (netted) pattern, and usually last for three or four weeks.

Those plants occurring naturally in high, cool areas need a minimum temperature of 52°F (11°C); those from lower, warmer, moister areas need 62°F (17°C). All require as much light as possible, without scorching, if they are to flower successfully; most require a short rest after flowering but water must not be stopped completely. The roots have a distinct green-brown tip that shows when the plant requires moisture. When this tip is covered over with the white velamen watering should be reduced.

Many hybrids, both terete and strap-leaved, have been produced. All require a minimum temperature of 62°F (17°C).

SPECIES

V. coerulea, from mountainous areas in India and Burma, is of a delightful shade of blue, with darker-blue veining and a dark lip. The broad-petalled flowers can be up to 4″ across, growing to 3′ high with 1″-wide, folded, V-shaped, strap-like leaves set very close together alternately on the stem. The flower spike, up to 18″ long, can carry up to fifteen flowers in the autumn for four to six weeks; it is inclined to lose its bottom leaves if watering is insufficient. The top, provided it has some aerial roots, can then be cut off and repotted; the old stump will sometimes produce new growths. Through selective breeding, many fine, deep-blue flowers are available.

V. coerulescens, a delightful species from Burma, has $\frac{1}{2}$″ pale-mauve flowers with a deep-blue lip. It is generally similar but smaller in growth than *V. coerulea*—it reaches up to 18″ high with 12″ spikes carrying up to eight long-lasting flowers in summer. The minimum night temperature must not be less than 52°F (11°C).

V. cristata is a charming plant, 12″ high, similar in growth to the above but with short, 6″ spikes carrying up to six green flowers, $\frac{1}{2}$″ in diameter. The lip is white, streaked with crimson-red. This plant comes from India, and flowers in the spring for about a month. Minimum temperature— 52°F (11°C).

V. teres has, as the name suggests, terete leaves; they are 6″ long, well-spaced on a thick woody stem. The leaves are the distinguishing feature of this plant, which can grow as high as 8′. Flower spikes up to 15″ long carry from eight to twenty flowers 3″ in diameter, white tinged with rose. The red lip is streaked yellow. The flowers are long-lasting, appearing in July and August. Coming as it does from the warm plains of India, this Vanda requires 62°F (17°C) with moist conditions.

Vanilla

Central America

This epiphytic orchid is the source of the vanilla flavouring used in ice cream, cakes etc. —a powder is made from the contents of the plant's seed pods. First used by the Incas, vanilla is now an important commercial crop in many tropical isles. The word 'vanilla' is Spanish for 'small pod'. Legend has it that it was first introduced into Spain in the form of pods in the early 1500s, and plants were introduced in the early 1700s. But although these plants flowered, they did not set seed as the insects required to pollinate them were not available in Europe. In 1838 Prof. C. Morren successfully pollinated the flowers artifically by hand and most commercially-grown plants are now pollinated this way.

The plant is a vigorous climber with dark-green stems up to 1″ thick. The thick, succulent leaves, 6″ long and 2″ wide, grow on alternate sides of the stem. Long aerial roots develop from many of the leaf joints, if the required humidity is present.

These plants are best grown in a temperature that does not drop below 65°F (18°C) with very moist conditions. Give it a stout pole to cling to. The flowers are similar to Cattleyas—3–5″ in diameter, coloured a very pretty, pale-green, with a yellow lip. They grow in small clusters of twos and threes, up to ten clusters on a short spike, a few opening each day.

If fertilised, the pods produced grow to about 6″ long and give off a delicious aroma when dried. They take eight or nine months to mature on the plant.

SPECIES

V. planifolia has thick, vine-like climbing stems $\frac{1}{2}$″ thick with fleshy leaves which grow to 6″. The greenish-yellow flowers are some 3″ across. This species comes from Mexico, and flowers in the summer for about a month.

9 More of a challenge

The orchids described in the last chapter should, with a little care, be successfully grown by the beginner. The ones described in the following pages are themselves not at all difficult, provided they are given the right conditions, particularly with regard to temperature. Temperatures within a greenhouse will often vary according to the position of the plant—you may be able to grow some of the warmer-growing species at one end, and still grow some of the cooler ones in another part of the greenhouse where it is more difficult to keep the temperature up.

Angraecum
Africa and Madagascar

Angraecums are handsome epiphytic orchids growing naturally on trees and mossy rocks. They require warm, shady conditions, a well-drained compost and plenty of moisture while growing. The flowers are usually green or white, and have a long spur containing nectar. The petals are waxy and firm. Some species are fragrant.

This is a monopodial genus, growing to heights ranging from 6″ to 4′. The thick, fleshy, long leaves are set close together; the roots are thick and mainly aerial. All the species described below need a temperature of at least 60°F (16°C).

SPECIES

A. eburneum grows up to 4′ high, with thick, fleshy leaves 18″ long, from six to twelve pale-green flowers with a broad, white lip and a greenish spur 3″ long and 2″ wide. It flowers in the spring. *A. eburneum* is a really beautiful plant, originating in Madagascar.

A. giryamae is a large plant, 3′ high, from Africa, with thick, fleshy leaves 12″ long and long aerial roots. It carries up to twenty pale-green star-shaped flowers, 3″ in diameter, with a large white lip and a 3″ spur. This is a very fragrant, summer-flowering species.

A. sesquipedale is a large plant growing to 3′ high, from Madagascar. It puts out many thick leaves 12″ long, and two or more glistening white flowers with a long, 15″ spur. When the species was first discovered,

Charles Darwin maintained that a moth or butterfly must exist with a tongue long enough to reach the nectar in the end of the spur. Many years later, the night-flying moth now known as *Xanthopan morgani 'praedicta'* was discovered. It has a 12″ proboscis, and when it was named the word 'praedicta' was included to commemorate Darwin's masterly prediction. The species flowers in the autumn (fall).

Leptotes

South America

This is a delightful, small-growing group of epiphytic orchids found growing naturally in clefts of branches. The pseudobulbs are small, each with a characteristic, round, terete leaf, 5″ across. Leptotes requires a fair amount of sunlight; it is best grown in pans or baskets. Flowers are star-shaped, lavender-pink in colour, very freely produced from the top of the pseudobulbs. The minimum growing temperature for this genus is 60°F (16°C). Do not over-water, and make sure drainage is effective, otherwise the pseudobulbs may tend to rot.

SPECIES

L. bicolor lives up to its name: the 2″ flowers are pale, pinky-white and the lip is darker purple. The plant grows to a height of 6″, with four or five flowers to a spike. It requires a temperature of at least 60°F (16°C), and flowers for about a month in May and June. Brazil is its country of origin.

L. unicolor has, as we would expect, flowers of one colour—pale lavender, and this includes the lip. Otherwise it is similar to *L. bicolor*.

Masdevallia

Central and South America

Masdevallias, which are among the most fascinating plants in the orchid world, are named in honour of the Spanish botanist Dr Masdeval. The flowers are strange, even weird in appearance, made up of three large, triangular sepals that often taper to tail-like appendages; sometimes the sepals are fused together. The petals and lip are usually tiny and insignificant. The fleshy leaves rise from a small creeping rhizome; they do not have pseudobulbs, and are almost stemless. Masdevallias are epiphytic, between 2″ and 18″ tall, and soon make large tufted plants.

Coming originally from cool, mountainous districts in Central and South America, the plants evolved in often misty conditions, and will tolerate a greenhouse temperature of 50°F (10°C), high humidity and

Paphiopedilum *Chipmunk 'Vermont'*, a typical hybrid variety, showing how selective breeding produces a fine, round-shaped flower with spectacular sepals and petals.

plenty of fresh, moving air. They do well growing in shade in a mixture of sphagnum moss and peat—they should not be allowed to dry out completely.

M. bella has 9″-high leaves, with long, drooping spikes carrying large, creamy-white flowers spotted with crimson. The tiny lip is white. The stem should be allowed to wither as a succession of flowers is produced from the same stem in summer. Brazil is its country of origin.

M. coccinea has dark-green leaves 8–9″ high, with long, 18″ flower spikes. The flowers are large, ranging in colour from rose-pink to brilliant magenta-purple with the bottom two sepals larger than the top, dorsal sepal. There are several varieties available of *M. coccinea*, which came originally from Colombia.

M. ignea is a beautiful orchid with lovely, single, scarlet-red flowers with crimson veining. Again, the tips of the sepals reflex into 2″-long tails, while the petals and lip are tiny. It flowers during the winter. Colombia is its place of origin.

M. tovarensis, from Venezuela, bears lovely white flowers, about 1″ in diameter, with short tails. There are usually two to a stem in winter.

Miltonia
Brazil and Colombia

Miltonia is known popularly as the 'pansy orchid'; it is so-called because of the flat pansy-like flowers. Miltonias are epiphytic, with small, flat pseudobulbs 3″ long and up to three 6″ leaves growing from each.

Be careful about the temperature—they need an equable 55°F (13°C) throughout the year, but also resent too much heat; they should not be allowed to dry out. Care must be taken not to spray the leaves, as being soft they are susceptible to spotting. Shade from strong sunlight.

M. candida from Brazil has 2″ pseudobulbs each carrying two 12″ leaves; the flower spikes are up to 18″ long, and carry five to seven $2\frac{1}{2}$″ yellowish-brown flowers with brown markings. The lip is white with purple spots. It flowers in the period from August to November.

M. spectabilis has usually single flowers, 3″ in diameter, creamy-white with a pinkish tinge, and dark purple blotches on the white lip. The

OPPOSITE
Phalaenopsis schilleriana.

colour can be very variable. The flowering time is July–August. This species has 3″ oval pseudobulbs on a creeping rhizome, and two leaves 6″ long on each.

M. vexillaria, from Colombia, has 2″ pseudobulbs with two leaves on top; other leaves stem from the base of the pseudobulbs. Twelve 18″-long flower spikes are freely produced, with from four to eight large flowers very variable in colour from light-rose to dark-rose, with an even darker lip streaked with yellow. This species has been used with others to produce the large, modern pansy-shaped hybrids, giving red, white, pink and yellow flowers.

Phalaenopsis
South-east Asia

This is a warm-growing epiphytic genus, commonly called the 'moth orchid', because its moth-like appearance attracts these animals for pollination. These plants need warm, humid conditions. Because they

Laelia purpurata, *one of the best Laelia species for the novice grower, with* 5″ *white flowers and a crimson-purple lip.*

*Two fine Paphiopedilums—*P. argus *and* P. barbatum, *showing typical formation and colour variation.*

have no pseudobulbs in which to store moisture, but only a short stem with large, fleshy leaves, they must not be allowed to dry out. Shady, humid conditions suit them best. Many beautiful hybrids have been produced in white, pink, yellow and striped varieties, with long arching flower spikes, sometimes branching and carrying up to a hundred long-lasting flowers up to 5″ in diameter. If the stem is cut back to a node after the flowers have died, another is produced within six months. A freely-drained, moist compost is required. A piece of bark is ideal.

P. amabilis has broad leaves 3″ wide and 6–10″ long. There are up to twenty flowers, 3″ across, and pure white in colour, with a white lip spotted red. The temperature must not drop below 65°F (18°C).

P. schilleriana is another broad-leaved species; the leaves are 3–4″ wide and some 12–18″ long, dark green marked with silver. The branched flower-spikes are 2′ 6″ long, and carry as many as thirty pinkish flowers, 3″ in diameter, with a white lip spotted pink. New plants often develop on the ends of the old spikes after flowering: when they are large enough and have developed their own roots, they may be severed and potted up independently. These plants, which need a temperature of at least 65°F

(18°C), do best hanging up in baskets so that the natural hanging habit of the flower stem is maintained. This also helps to stop water collecting in the crown of the plant, which can lead to the development of rot. The long aerial roots should be allowed to hang and take up moisture from the atmosphere.

Promenaea
Brazil

This is a cool-growing, epiphytic orchid, a dwarf plant ideal for a plantarium. It has small, shiny pseudobulbs 1″ in length, with soft, grey-green leaves which grow to 2″ long. The flowers are freely produced in summer on 2″ wiry stems and are up to 2″ across, yellow in colour. They last about two weeks. A minimum of 55°F (18°C) suits this genus, with moist shady conditions.

SPECIES

P. citrina will soon fill a pot with its small, soft leaves. The flowers are 1½″ in diameter, and 1″ deep. The colour is a clear lemon-yellow; the lip is spotted with red.

P. stapelioides has pale-yellow flowers, heavily marked with reddish-brown bars; the lip is much darker.

Stanhopea
Central America

Named in honour of the Earl of Stanhope, this genus has flowers that are one of nature's most bizarre creations, almost impossible to describe. Growers tend either to love them or hate them. When first introduced it grew for many years without flowering, until it was discovered that the flowers and stem grew downwards, and therefore could not get out of the pots they were being grown in. When put in baskets the flowers push out from the base of the pseudobulbs through the compost. The buds, when ready to open, explode with a distinctive popping noise.

Flowers are very large, 3–8″, and there are from four to eight on a stem, yellow in colour. Most are scented, although not to everyone's taste. So, these plants must be grown in baskets, and hung up near the glass. Ample moisture is needed when growing. But care must be taken, when flowers are due, so as to avoid rotting the spikes developing in the compost. Rest plants from October to December.

S. tigrina has 3″ oval pseudobulbs topped by a large, broad single plicate leaf on a 3–5″ stem. The flowers are creamy-yellow with blood-red blotches, and are 6″ in diameter. There are up to six on an 18″ spike in July–August and they are quite fragrant, lasting for two or three days. It requires a minimum temperature of 60°F (16°C). Mexico is its natural home.

S. wardii, from Guatemala, is similar to *S. tigrina*, except that it has a longer flower spike with up to eight yellow flowers, 3″ in diameter and marked with reddish-purple spots. This one, too, flowers in the summer, and needs a temperature of 60°F (16°C). It comes from Guatemala.

Questions and answers to common problems

Q   What makes the tips of roots of orchids go black and die back?
A   Check the water for impurities, and the fertiliser for strength. If it is too strong it will burn the roots.

Q   Why will the roots of some plants not stay in the pot, preferring to grow outside?
A   The roots of epiphytic orchids (these are fully described earlier in the book) take most of their nourishment from the atmosphere. So do not damage the roots by trying to force them into the compost. Leave them alone.

Q   Why are ants sometimes particularly active on certain plants?
A   Ants will often nest in compost, especially if it is kept too dry. This often happens with plants in the more inaccessible parts of the greenhouse, because these can be often missed when you water your collection. Ants do not actually cause harm of themselves, but they do transport aphids and other sap-feeding pests from plant to plant. Prevention is better than cure here—the only way of dealing with ants once they are on the plant is with a spray-on insecticide, although this is not always effective. It is far better to kill them where they nest.

Q   What is the black, mould-like substance that sometimes appears on leaves?
A   This is a sweet, honey-like substance secreted by aphids etc. Ants are particularly fond of it. Wash it off with warm, soapy water and cotton-wool, and check the plant for insects.

Q   Why are the leaves on some new growths crinkly in appearance, and unable to open properly?
A   This problem is usually caused by faulty watering leading to a check in growth. The plant is being kept either too wet or too dry.

Q   How long should a flower be left on a plant?
A   It depends on the genus. Cymbidiums and Paphiopedilums should be cut about three weeks after they have opened fully. Placed in water, the flowers should then last for a further four or five weeks. The flowers of most other genera should be cut as soon as they begin to wither. Remember to dust all cut stems with sulphur powder. Flowers on large, strong, seedling plants should be cut within seven days; but hard though it may seem, any flowers that develop on small seedling plants should be nipped off as soon as they are large enough to handle. This is to relieve the plant of the strain of carrying the flowers, and to allow it to build up a strong growth capable of flowering well the next year.

Q   Some old, damaged or dead leaves are sometimes difficult to remove by pulling off. What is the best method in such cases?
A   Split the leaf down the centre vein first; then pull each piece away from the split. It should come away easily without causing damage to either bulb or growth.

Q   When is the best time to repot?
A   Most healthy plants are repotted when fresh new roots are seen to appear at the base. The potting should be carried out before these roots are $\frac{1}{2}''$ long. Any sickly plant should be potted in fresh compost immediately you notice its condition, and placed in a shady, moist position until new roots appear. Great care must be taken with watering—it is best to spray the plant lightly each day until the new roots have reached a length of $\frac{1}{2}''$, at which stage normal watering can begin.

Q   Why do leaves turn yellow and fall off the plant?
A   This happens in autumn (fall), and usually happens on old back-bulbs. It is usually a quite natural process.

Q   Why do buds drop off plants before they have opened?
A   Some plants resent over-high temperatures in the autumn–winter period—unfortunately this is the time when control is sometimes most difficult. Cool-growing plants like Cymbidiums resent any rise much above 55°F (13°C) at this time. The same symptoms can also be caused by a too-dry atmosphere.

Q   What makes flowers on Cymbidiums turn a pinkish-red colour after they have been open for a day or so?
A   The colour change suggests that the flower has been pollinated by a bee, or some such visitor. Check the doors and ventilators of your orchid house for gaps that allow the entry of insects.

Q   Why are some flowers and flower buds twisted?
A   The plant has probably been moved while the spike was developing. All growths develop towards the light, which means they will quite likely change direction if moved so that the light comes from a different angle.

Q   How does one get the mycorrhiza fungus into newly potted plants?
A   The fungus is already there, present in the plants' roots and leaves, and it soon permeates the new compost.

Glossary

Apart from technical English terms used in the text, the list also contains many of the Latin names used to describe species, including some that are not used in this book, but which you may well come across in catalogues.

Certain Latin words which are given here with the masculine ending will also be found with the feminine or neuter endings. The meaning is not affected. The names derived from proper names are not included.

acaulis with no stem
adventitious of shoots, appearing in unusual places
aerial growing into the air, rather than into the pot
aggregata side-by-side
albidus whitish
albino white, without colour
albus white
alifolius wing-like
amabilis beautiful
amethystoglossus with an amethyst-coloured lip
ampliatus very large
anceps double-edged
angustifolius narrow-leaved
anther pollen-bearing part of a stamen
apical at the tip of a plant or growth
apiferus like a bee
argentus silvery-coloured
aromaticus sweet-smelling
asymbiotic of the raising of seed, without the use of fungus, artificial
aureus golden-yellow
autropurpureus dark-purple
autrorubens dark-red
autumnalis flowering in autumn (fall)
axil angle between leaf and stem

back bulb old, leafless pseudobulb with dormant eye, used for new growth
barbatus with beard, as barley
bicolor two-coloured
brachiatus branched

bract leaves round base of flower, usually brownish
bractescens with large bract

calcareous alkaline
calceolate slipper-like
calyx outer covering of flower buds
caudatus having thin, long petals
cembolletus having thin, rush-like leaves
cernuus hanging, drooping
chlorophyll green colouring matter, enabling the use of light energy in the manufacture of food for a plant
chlorosis the lack of chlorophyll
chrysotoxum with golden sprays
ciliaris fringed with hairs
cinnabarina coloured red
citratus yellow, lemon coloured
citrinus yellow, lemon coloured
cochleatus shell-like in shape
coeruleus sky-blue
coerulescens bluish, becoming blue
column organ formed by the combination, peculiar to orchids, of stamen and pistil
concolor uniform in colour
cordatus having a heart-shaped lip
crispus with a curled or crisped lip
cristatus crested
cucullatus hooded
cultivar special cultivated form of a species or hybrid plant

delicatus delicate
densiflorus with dense clusters of flowers
dorsal of petal or sepal, 'back' (adj.)

elatus tall
elegans elegant
ensifolius with sword-shaped leaves
epiphytic living in air, perhaps attached to another plant, but deriving no substance from it
eye dormant growth of flower bud at base of plant that can start to grow

falcated shaped like a scythe
fir bark chopped or ground bark of tree

flaccidus drooping
flexuosus twisted
fragrans sweet-scented
frimbriatus fringed

genera plural form of genus, see below
genus classification applied to a group of botani-
    cally similar plants
giganteus gigantic or large
gigas gigantic or large
glaucus blue-green in colour
gracilis graceful
grandiflorus large-flowered
grandifolius large-leaved
grandis grand or large
granulosus granular
guttatus spotted

hirsutissimus very hairy
hybrid a cross between two plants of different
    genera, species or varieties

igneus bright crimson
incurvus curved or bent inwards
infundibularis funnel-shaped
insignis distinctive
intergeneric of a cross, between two different
    genera
intermedius intermediate
internodal between leaf joints

juncifolius with rush-like leaves

laevis smooth, very even
lanceolate lance-shaped, pointed
latifolius broad-leaved
leucochilus white-lipped
linguiformis tongue-shaped
lip modified petal
longifolius long-leaved
luridus straw-brown
luteolus pale-yellow
lutescens yellowish, becoming yellow

macranthus large-flowered
macrochilus large-lipped

macrophyllus large-leaved
maculatus spotted
majalis flowering in May
majus large
marginatus with the edge a different colour
maximus largest
meleagris spotted
microchilus small-lipped
moniliformis thin and chain-like
monocotyledon plant whose seedling produces
    only one leaf
monopodial of single growth extending up-
    wards each year
moschatus musk-scented
mosciferus like a fly
multiflora many-flowered
multigeneric of a cross, of more than one genus
mycorrhiza fungus that invades seed and root
    of orchid and feeds it

niveus white, whitish
node joint on stem where leaf is attached

ochraceus ochre-yellow
oculatus with an eye-like mark
odoratus scented
ornithorhynchus beak-shaped
ovoid egg-shaped

panduratus fiddle-shaped
papilio butterfly-like
plicate of leaves, folded like the bellows of an
    accordion
polybulbus many-bulbed
praecox early-flowering
proliferate produce offshoots
pseudobulb false-bulb-like stem that stores food
pulchellus dainty
pumilus low-growing
purpuratus purple-marked

raft flat piece of bark, wood or tree fern on
    which to grow plant
rhizome creeping rootstock above or below
    ground joining pseudobulbs or leaf stems
rhodostictus marked with red

rubescens reddish
rupestris growing in rocky places or on rocks

saprophyte deriving food from dead organic matter
sarcodes fleshy, waxy in texture
scandens climbing
sepal each segment of calyx
sesquipedalis measuring a foot and a half
spathulatus spoon or spatula-shaped
species botanical group of plants with common characteristics
speciosus handsome
stamen male pollen-bearing organ
stellatus star-shaped
suavis sweetly scented
superbus superb
symbiosis living together of different organisms, where both benefit

tenuifolius slender-leaved
terete shape of long, thin, cylindrical leaf
thyrsiflorus with flower-clusters like bunches of grapes
tigrinus tiger-like
tortilis twisted
tricolor three-coloured

velutinus velvety
venustum elegant
verrucosus with wart-like appendages
vexillarius upright, of military bearing
villosus with long, soft hairs
virginalis white

xanthinus yellow

COMMON ABBREVIATIONS FOR AWARDS

AM	Award of Merit
BC	Botanical Certificate
BM	Bronze Medal
BMC	Bronze Medal Certificate
CBM	Certificate of Botanical Merit
CC	Certificate of Culture
CPC	Certificate of Preliminary Commendation
FCC	First Class Certificate
GM	Gold Medal
HCC	Highly Commended Certificate
JC	Judges' Commendation
PC	Preliminary Commendation
SM	Silver Medal

COMMON ABBREVIATIONS FOR AWARDING BODIES

AOC	Australian Orchid Council
AOS	American Orchid Society
CSA	Cymbidium Society of America
HSO	Honolulu Orchid Society
MNEOS	Manchester and North of England Orchid Society
MOS	Malayan Orchid Society
NSW	Orchid Society of New South Wales
NZOS	New Zealand Orchid Society
ODC	Orchid Digest Corporation
OSGB	Orchid Society of Great Britain
OSSC	Orchid Society of Southern California
RHS	Royal Horticultural Society
SFOS	South Florida Orchid Society
VIC	Victoria Orchid Club

National societies

AUSTRALIA
Australian Orchid Council
15 Bayfield Place, Bayview, N.S.W. 2104,
Australia.

AUSTRIA
Österreichische Orchideen-Gesellschaft
Singerstr. 27, A-1010 Wien, Austria.

BELGIUM
Belgian Orchid Society
Driesstraat 12, 9231 Controde, Belgium.

BRAZIL
Sociedade Brasileiro do Orquidofilos
Caixa Postal 4714, Rio de Janeiro, Brazil.

COLOMBIA
Sociedad Colombiana de Orquideologia
a.p. Aereo 4725, Medellin, Colombia.

DENMARK
Denmark Orchid Club
Dyrlaege 4174, Jystrup, Denmark.

FRANCE
Société Française d'Orchidophilie
c/o 5 Rue de Paris, 94470, Boissy-St-Leger,
France.

GREAT BRITAIN
Orchid Society of Great Britain
28 Felday Road, Lewisham, London SE13 7HJ,
England.

HAWAII
Hawaiian Orchid Society
84-839 Mena St, Waianae, Oahu,
Hawaii, 96792.

ITALY
Associazione Italiana per la Orchidee
Via Dante 11, 25100, Brescia, Italy.

JAMAICA
Jamaican Orchid Society
Wai Rua Road, Gorden Town P.O., Kingston 7,
Jamaica.

JAPAN
Japanese Orchid Society
2.27 Doshu-Cho, Higashiku, Osaka City, Japan.

KENYA
Kenya Orchid Society
P.O. Box 241, Nairobi, Kenya.

MEXICO
Ass. Mexicana de Orquideologia
Apalado Postal 53-123, 17 DF, Mexico.

NETHERLANDS
Nederlandse Orchideen Vereniging
Emmastraat 14, Aalsmeer, Netherlands.

PORTUGAL
Portuguese Orchid Society
R.S. Caetane 2, Lisbon, Portugal.

RHODESIA
Rhodesian Orchid Society
Box 8196, Causeway, Salisbury, Rhodesia.

SWEDEN
Swedish Orchid Society
Helsingborgsvagen 22, S-26200, Sweden.

SWITZERLAND
Schweizerische Orchideengesellschaft
Ch-9053, Teufen, Switzerland.

USA
American Orchid Society
Botanical Museum of Harvard University,
Cambridge, Mass. 02138, USA.

WEST GERMANY
Deutsche Orchideen-Gesellschaft
Bornemaunstrasse 2, Frankfurt, W. Germany.

Bibliography

Ames and Correll. *Orchids of Guatemala.* 1953.

Blowers, J. W. *Pictorial Orchid Growing.* Maidstone, 1966.

Briscow, T. W. *Orchids for Amateurs*, 2nd ed. London, 1946.

Curtis, C. H. *Orchids for Everyone.* London and New York, 1910.

Curtis, C. H. *Orchids: Their Description and Cultivation.* London, 1950.

Darwin, A. *The Various Contrivances by which Orchids are Fertilised by Insects,* 2nd ed. London, 1899.

Dunsterville, G. C. K. *Introduction to the World of Orchids.* London, 1964.

Duperrex, A. *Orchids of Europe* (translated from the French by A. J. Huxley). London, 1961.

Eigeldinger, O. and Murphy, L. S. *Orchids.* London, 1971.

Freed, H. *Orchids and Serendipity.* New Jersey, 1970.

Hawkes, A. D. *Cultural Directions for Orchids* (part 1). Florida, 1959.

Hawkes, A. D. *Orchids, Their Botany and Culture.* London, 1961.

Hawkes, A. D. *Encyclopedia of Cultivated Orchids.* London and New York, 1965.

Lecoufle, N. and Rise, H. *Orchids.* London, 1957

MacDonald, N. *The Orchid Hunters.* London, 1942.

McKensie Black, P. *Beautiful Orchids.* London, 1973.

Montes de Oca. *Humming Birds and Orchids of Mexico.* Mexico, 1963.

Nelson, W. H. *Orchids of Australia.* Melbourne, 1969.

Noble, M. *You Can Grow Orchids.* Florida, 1960.

Noble, M. *You Can Grow Phalaenopsis Orchids.* Florida, 1971.

Northern, R. T. *Orchids as House Plants.* Toronto, New York and London, 1950.

Northern, R. T. *Home Orchid Growing.* New York, 1970.

Reinikka, M. A. *A History of the Orchid.* Florida, 1973.

Richter, W. *The Orchid World.* London, 1965.

Richter, W. *Orchid Care.* London, 1972.

Rittershausen, P. R. C. *Successful Orchid Culture.* London and New York, 1953.

Rittershausen, B. and W. *Popular Orchids.* Newton Abbot, 1970.

Russen, A. and Boyle, F. *The Orchid Seekers.* London, c. 1896.

Sander, C. F. and L. L. *Sanders Orchid Guide.* St. Albans, 1927.

Sander, D. F. *Orchids and their Cultivation.* London, 1969.

Schultes, R. E. *Native Orchids of Trinidad and Tobago.* Oxford, 1960.

Summerhayes, V. S. *Wild Orchids of Britain.* London, 1951.

Swinson, A. *The Orchid King.* London, 1970.

Veitch, J. and sons. *A Manual of Orchidaceous Plants.* London, 1887–94.

Williams, B. S. *The Orchid Grower's Manual.* London, 1894.

Withner, C. L. *The Orchids: A Scientific Survey.* New York, 1959.

Most societies throughout the world publish their own journals and bulletins; the oldest independently published orchid periodical (there are still very few of them) is *The Orchid Review*, published in Great Britain.

Picture acknowledgements

Page numbers given, those in italics refer to colour.

A-Z Botanical Collections Limited, Dorking: *10*, *47*, *66*, *74*, *78*, *98*, *99*. Ernest L. Crowson F.R.P.S.: 14, 62, *107*. Author's photographs: 18, 26, *35*, *42*, 48, *79*, 85, *102*, *110*. E. W. Self: 29, *39*. Kuno Kreiger, Herdecke-Ende, Germany: 41, 44. Royston J. Dunn: 58, *71* (flower owned by Mrs G. Cotton). Brian Furner: *111*.

Index

Page numbers referring to the captions of colour illustrations are given in **bold**; those referring to the captions of black and white illustrations, or the labelling within a diagram, are given in *italic*. Selected orchids are described in detail on pages 67–113; their names are listed here, but references to botanical features and growing conditions in that section are not listed as they occur throughout it.